MORE THRILLING WESTERN STORIES

(each with a gospel application)

BY

Evangelist Bill Rice, D.D.; D.S.T.; Hum. D.

Faith Baptist Church Publications
3607 Oleander Avenue
Fort Pierce, Florida 34982

FOREWORD
by
Cathy Rice

Bill Rice was a unique personality. My grandmother always said, "After Bill Rice was made, the mold was broken." This, not because she thought he was a tremendous person with great ability, but because he was all legs.

Bill Rice stood six feet, two inches, straight, tall and erect. He always walked briskly with an air of authority. You had the feeling he knew exactly where he was going and what he planned to do. Though Bill Rice was an evangelist for thirty-seven years, he always said he was probably more at home in the saddle than in the pulpit. Born and reared in the ranch country of West Texas, he was breaking horses by the time he was thirteen. Riding, camping, hunting and fishing were -- for as long as he could remember -- a way of life for him.

BILL RICE WAS AN EVANGELIST

Bill Rice was a full-time evangelist! In his mid-twenties, as he was first starting his ministry, he pastored a small church in Gainesville, Texas, for three years. It was during this time he married Catherine Widner. He also became aware of the fact that he needed more training for his ministry. Although he had worked his way through a Baptist college in Texas, he felt his need for Bible training.

He and his wife and their first child, left the warm climate of Texas to go to the cold and snowy climate of Chicago to attend the Moody Bible Institute just before Christmas of 1937. While attending Moody, he established and pastored a church in Dubuque, Iowa. He pastored this church also for three years.

HIS FIRST LOVE

Revival campaigns were his first love, so upon graduation from Moody in August of 1941 he immediately entered into full-time evangelism and this he did for thirty-seven years until his death in May of 1978.

Bill Rice, however, was a very busy man and added many facets to his ministry. He served on several mission boards, edited a cowboy Christian paper called <u>The Branding Iron</u>, managed a summer campground, conducted a weekly radio broadcast, was co-editor of <u>The Sword of the Lord</u>, and authored several books and gospel songs. Among his books -- his most famous are <u>"Cowboy Boots in Darkest Africa"</u> and <u>"Love 'em, Lick 'em and Learn 'em."</u>

Each chapter in the book, <u>"Cowboy Boots in Darkest Africa"</u> is filled with excitement and thrilling stories of his time spent in the old Belgian Congo. He went there in January of 1951 to help missionaries establish a Pygmy church. Each chapter is packed with exciting stories of events that happened while in the Congo and each chapter ends with a gospel application.

Another well-known book is <u>"Love 'em, Lick 'em and Learn 'em"</u> on raising children. To me, this is by far one of the best books on child rearing ever printed. The first chapter, however, is on marriage. Bill had an unusual knack for putting on paper God's admonition to us. It will do any marriage good to read this chapter.

THE COLORFUL BILL RICE RANCH

Perhaps the most unique phase of Dr. Rice's ministry was the work he did with his wife, Cathy, among those who cannot hear.

They founded the Bill Rice Ranch, the world's largest independent missionary work to the Deaf. They not only conducted (Cathy still does) a school teaching Sign Language to the hearing, but Deaf teenagers from all over the United States, and often from foreign countries, come to the Ranch each summer.

FROM A HEARTBREAK

The Rices were heartbroken to learn that their firstborn, Betty, was deafened when she was near two years of age by meningitis. Dr. Bill was the father of two daughters, two sons and an adopted deaf son. They are Betty, Kaye, Bill III, Pete and Ronnie.

Dr. Bill was blessed of God in revivals throughout America and in other countries. But he and his wife were concerned that Betty "see" the Gospel of Christ. The Rices took much time and work to show Betty that God loved her and that Christ died for her. You can understand the joy in their hearts as Betty trusted Christ at the age of eight after seeing God's love through "visual aids, homemade signs and an old blackboard."

Bill Rice soon learned, however, that there were millions of Deaf in America that needed to "see" the Gospel. Dr. Rice and his wife thought it would be good if they could build a small camp where Deaf could come -- perhaps fifteen or twenty at a time -- and see the wonderful story of Christ.

He was able to locate an old worn-out, run-down ranch near Murfreesboro, Tennessee, in 1950 while conducting a three-week revival campaign. The ranch had lain dormant for forty years but was steeped in the romance of by-gone days. The 1,300-acre ranch encircled part of an old Pioneer settlement, two graveyards more than 100 years old and Indian altars. Today fine horses graze where deer and other game once roamed freely and the camp, which was filled to capacity with twelve Deaf its first summer, has grown to a world-wide ministry. Hundreds of Deaf and hearing come each year to have a good time and fellowship around the Word of God.

Today, the Bill Rice Ranch is the world's largest camp for the Deaf and the South's biggest independent conference ground. Each summer preachers, families and teenagers come from many states to have the time of their lives. They swim, hike, ride beautiful horses, enter the weekly rodeo, play softball, or just plain loaf. Best of all, they fellowship with other Christians. Hundreds of Deaf and hearing, down through the years, have been saved.

ALWAYS BUSY

Whether you found Dr. Rice riding a rugged mountain trail with a week's growth of beard on his face, boots on his feet, gun by his side and lead rope in his hand; or working as a cowboy on his own 1,300-acre ranch in middle Tennessee, or preaching in a revival campaign, you probably noticed he was -- to use his own words -- "gettin' a lot of livin' out of life."

And that is exactly what he did until God saw fit to take him to Glory.

ACKNOWLEDGMENT.

We wish to acknowledge the kind and generous spirit of Mrs. Cathy Rice (Dr. Bill's wife) and Dr. Bill Rice, III, who have graciously consented to the publication of this wonderful book.

All the stories in this edition were taken from *"The Branding Iron"* as they appeared over the last many years. *"The Branding Iron"* is published by Bill Rice Ranch in Murfreesboro, Tennessee.

May these stories continue to bless the hearts of thousands as the voice of Bill Rice "still speaks."

CONTENTS

TAKEN FOR A RIDE BY GANGSTERS

THE TRUE STORY OF THE DAY BILL RICE PREACHED THE FUNERAL OF CHICAGO GANGSTER'S WIFE — AND WAS TAKEN FOR A RIDE BY ARMED GUNSTERS. THE CONVERSATION CONCERNED — OF ALL THINGS — THE VIRGIN MARY!

The Catholic Church teaches many things about the Virgin Mary that simply are not true.

For example, it is Catholic dogma that Mary was born without a sinful nature and lived a completely sinless life. They call this the "Immaculate Conception." They believe that Mary was born as a result of a union between her father and mother. But they also believe that the very second her soul and body were united in her mother's womb, God miraculously prevented her from inheriting the sinful nature of Adam's race and she was sinlessly perfect until the day of her death.

Of course this is absolutely contrary to the plain teaching of the Scripture. As a matter of fact, Mary herself confessed that she was a sinner who needed salvation. She said,

"...My soul doth magnify the Lord, And my spirit hath rejoiced in God my Saviour." (Luke 1:46,47).

Mary needed a Saviour like everyone else because she, too, was a sinner.

Again, Catholics teach that Mary was the "Mother of God" and as such has more influence with Jesus than anyone else. Therefore, we ought to pray and ask her to intercede with her Son for us. But this, too, is absolutely contrary to the teaching of the Bible. It is true that Mary was the mother of Jesus. But it is not true that she has any special influence over Him. One day when Jesus was preaching, His mother and His brothers came and wished to speak with Him. Read the brief account in Matthew 12:47-50.

"Then one said unto him, Behold, thy mother and thy brethren stand without, desiring to speak with thee. But he

answered and said unto him that told him, Who is my mother? and who are my brethren? And he stretched forth his hand toward his disciples, and said, Behold my mother and my brethren! For whosoever shall do the will of my Father which is in heaven, the same is my brother, and sister, and mother."

Jesus made it very plain that, in a spiritual relationship, His mother and His brothers were no closer to Him than any other saved person who is trying to do the will of God.

The idea that God is so busy that we had better pray to Mary or one of the other "saints" and get them to do some lobbying with the Heavenly Father is pure nonsense.

Then there is a legend that has grown into Catholic doctrine that Mary did not molder in the grave but was resurrected and taken into Heaven. Catholics call this the "Assumption of Mary." Again they have no Scripture at all. Their argument is that death is a result of sin and Mary was not a sinner; therefore, she did not see corruption.

Actually, Mary was a sinner saved by grace just like every other Christian who has ever been saved. She lived and she died, and her body, right this minute, awaits the Resurrection Day along with my parents and every other Christian who has died in the Lord.

Nevertheless, Mary was an unusual and blessed woman. I preached on something she said at the funeral of a gangster's wife one time — and was taken for a ride as a result!

A Woman's Funeral

I was a student at the Moody Bible Institute. It was during the summer vacation, and most students had gone home. Cathy and I had no home, however, except the little dingy basement room near the school where we lived. One day someone from the institute called and asked me to come as quickly as possible. I was told that the director of a funeral home could not get a preacher to preach a funeral and had called upon the institute for help. It seemed that a Catholic woman had married a Jewish man and so neither a Jewish rabbi nor a Catholic priest was willing to officiate at the funeral. Since I was an ordained Baptist preacher and since none of the faculty were available, the school wanted me to go.

There was no time to prepare a message. I dashed home, and while I put on a clean shirt the Princess ironed my suit, and I was on my way.

When I arrived at the funeral chapel I was rather amazed at all the expensive automobiles — Cadillacs, Lincolns, and Chryslers were parked everywhere. And I was surprised at something else — the director of the establishment. He was a rather slender, bald-headed man who was shaking like the proverbial leaf and mopping sweat from his bald head and face. He was waiting for me and nervously took me into a small room at the back of the chapel. He asked me if I knew anything about the funeral and I told him I did not. He told me the name of the woman who had died and it still did not ring a bell with me. He asked me if I hadn't read the newspapers and I told him no, I couldn't afford one. (Absolutely true!)

Briefly the undertaker filled me in. The chapel was filled with gangsters. Not only gangsters but from two rival gangs. The dead woman was the daughter of one gangster and her husband was an "enforcer" (gunman) on the rival gang. The two gangs were at war, and each had killed men on the other side.

But this wasn't all — the woman had been a Catholic, and her husband was a Jew. Her parents had insisted that a Catholic priest officiate at the funeral, and the husband had insisted that a rabbi conduct the funeral. When they discovered they could find neither priest nor rabbi who would take the job, both sides were even more furious.

As the undertaker talked with me and mopped his head he was as frightened, I believe, as any man I have ever seen. He was scared half to death. He was afraid that war would break out during the funeral and that all of us might be killed. When I ridiculed the idea that anyone would actually do such a thing at a funeral, he opened the door a crack and told me to look at all the men wearing guns.

I looked and — this is going to be hard for you to believe, but upon my word of honor it is absolutely the truth — I saw big bulges near the left armpit of almost every man in the chapel! In some cases a man would have his coat unbuttoned, and I could actually see the leather strap running across the chest attached to the shoulder holster.

There was no question about it — these fellows actually were packing enough hardware to make a National Guard unit look like a troop of Boy Scouts!

And there was no doubt about this, either — they were the toughest, meanest, maddest-looking group I had ever seen. Although there were a few women in the crowd, most of them were men.

"Don't Mention Christ"

"Make your sermon brief," the director told me. "Just say she was a wonderful woman and say some beautiful things about death and let it go at that. Whatever you do, don't mention Christ."

Great Guns! By this time I was about as scared as he was and I was about as mad as the fellows sitting in the chapel. I was sore at the Moody Bible Institute for getting me into a spot like this!

But scared or not, I was still a preacher of the Gospel, and I told the director I would not preach any message that was not about Jesus Christ, and I would not pray any prayer that I did not pray in His Name. Unless that was clearly understood, I was gonna walk right out into the chapel, tell the people that I would not preach the service and tell them why, and then I was gonna put my Bible under my arm and high-tail it for home!

He argued and I stood firm. I would make the message brief, but it was going to be about Jesus Christ or there would be no message at all. In the meantime, the crowd in the chapel was getting restless, as we could see through the slightly opened door. Ole Baldy had to do something, and he didn't have all day to decide what it was, either. So he walked out into the chapel, said something to the husband of the dead woman, and the two of them came back to the little room where I was. I told him that the director had insisted that I not mention Jesus Christ, but that I was a Baptist preacher. Immediately the man's anger flared. He called Jesus a "bastard" and said if I even mentioned Him there would be "Hell to pay."

I replied that it was not his funeral but his wife's funeral. He might hate Jesus, but she had been a Catholic who had professed faith in Christ. No matter what he thought of Jesus, she would want me to talk about Him.

To my surprise he was convinced! After a few minutes, he agreed that I should preach the message, as best I knew, in a way that would please his wife whether he and his friends liked it or not. He asked, however, that we not start the service until he had time to sell the other Jews on the idea.

We watched as he went back into the chapel and went from man to man, explaining what he had decided and earnestly asking that no one start trouble.

The Message

It was not until the service began with some kind of organ music that I suddenly realized I hadn't the least idea in the world as to what I was going to say! I hastily prayed for wisdom and almost immediately God gave me a message.

I began by saying that a funeral is always sad because our hearts are broken over the loss of a loved one. But this funeral was sad not only because of bereavement but because of the bitterness and hatred in their hearts toward one another. I went on to say that I realized the condition was worse because some were Jews and some Catholics but that God had given me an unusual message for this occasion, and asked that they give me a chance to be of genuine help to them. During this introduction, their faces were hard as stone.

Turning to the Jews, I said I believed God had honored the Hebrew nation among all the peoples on the earth. I spoke briefly of Abraham, the friend of God. I spoke of Isaac, obedient unto death. I spoke of Jacob, who became Israel, and of David, the king.

But had they, I wondered, ever heard of a wonderful Jewish girl, a true daughter of Abraham, whom God had blessed above all the women on the earth? She was a Hebrew girl of whom Abraham, Isaac and Jacob, Moses, David, and Daniel would have been very proud.

The name of this lovely Jewish girl was — Mary.

What Mary Said

By this time everyone in the room was listening intently. As I spoke of the great Hebrew heroes of the Old Testament, the Jews were pleased. I have known some Jews who were as vile and wicked as the Devil could wish, but I have never in all my life known a Jew who did not take pride in his kinship to Abraham.

When I mentioned Mary's name, the Catholics came alive. Even though some Catholics may not worship Mary, all of them love and honor her even as the Jews do Abraham.

I went on to show that his Jewish girl, Mary, was highly honored by being the one God selected to give birth to His Son — she was the virgin mentioned in Isaiah 7:14:

"Therefore the Lord himself shall give you a sign; Behold a virgin shall conceive, and bear a son, and shall call his name Immanuel."

And what could we learn from this Jewish maid, the Virgin Mary? Well, at the wedding in Cana, she said, concerning Jesus, **"Whatsoever he saith unto you, do it."**

A Jewish girl, speaking to both Jews and Christians, said we should pay attention to Jesus and do whatever He tells us to do.

Jesus Said...

I mentioned a number of things that Jesus said, but I stressed only two of them.

First, Jesus said to Nicodemus, a ruler of the Jews, **"Ye must be born again."** It was not enough that Nicodemus was a son of Abraham. He must be born again if he is to see the Kingdom of God. A Hebrew, without the New Birth, can go to Hell just as quick as an Englishman, African or Chinaman.

Second, Jesus commanded that men should believe on Him. He said very plainly in John 14:6,

"I am the way, the truth, and the life: no man cometh unto the Father, but by me."

No one will go to Heaven, then, because he believes in the Virgin Mary! No one is going to be saved because of some priest saying the Mass or hearing confession or granting indulgences!

There is just one way for both Jews and Gentiles, for Protestants and Catholics and Jews — and that one way is Jesus Christ.

At the end of the brief message, many of those hardened gangsters (honestly I could say "most") were weeping. I asked them to reverently bow their heads in prayer and asked how many wanted me to pray for them. Hands were raised all over the chapel.

Taken For a Ride By Gangsters — Twice!

At the close of the service the funeral director, greatly relieved, expressed his appreciation and told me I might ride to the cemetery with him. I turned to follow him outside when the father of the dead woman grabbed me by the arm and said, "I want you to ride with me."

I quickly agreed. After all...

I rode in the front seat between the driver and this man. Armed gunmen crowded into the back seat of the limousine. On the way to the cemetery, he asked me if his daughter was in Heaven, Hell or purgatory. I told him there was no such place as purgatory, and that the only thing I could definitely tell him was that his daughter was in the hands of a just God. But I could also tell him that, no matter where his daughter was, she would want him to follow the advice of the Virgin Mary and turn to Christ.

There was a very brief and simple service at the graveside. The funeral director then told me that I might ride back with him. As I followed him to his car, a man again clutched my arm. I turned and found it was the husband of the dead woman and another man.

"We would like for you to ride back with us."

Again, I was quick to agree. Again I got into the front seat of a limousine. I sat between the driver and the husband, while the back seat was filled with armed thugs. On the ride back, the young husband asked almost the same question that the woman's father had asked. He wanted to know where his wife was. Evidently he really had loved her very much. Again I went over the gospel plan of salvation as they drove me back to the Moody Bible Institute. I had prayer with them, and they drove away, leaving me standing on the curb.

It was certainly one of the strangest experiences of my entire life. And it was one of the most blessed ones. Of course I cannot know what goes on in the hearts of men, but when I get to Heaven, I will not be surprised if I find that some of those gangsters turned from their lives of crime that day to salvation in the Lord Jesus Christ.

And with all the sincerity of my heart, I urge that you, too, trust Jesus today to forgive your sins and save your soul.

A Tale Of Two Horses

A TRUE STORY OF TWO WILD HORSES THAT WERE TRAINED THE SAME SUMMER. ONE HAD UNUSUAL SPEED, STAMINA AND ABILITY...AND YET WAS ALMOST WORTHLESS! IT WAS THE LESSER HORSE THAT BECAME AN OUTSTANDING ONE.

I cannot remember when I learned to ride a horse any more than I can remember just when I first learned to walk. I have literally been doing both since before I can remember. I was born on a ranch near Dundee, Texas, and my earliest memories are of my father putting me up on his cow pony and letting me ride by myself from the house to the barn.

When I was four years old, we moved to the little town of Decatur, Texas. Dad sold all of our stock except Flossie, my mother's beautiful blood-bay saddle mare. (My mother, an excellent horsewoman, rode sidesaddle. I can still remember seeing her ride that big bay in a dead run.)

But we had about ten acres behind our house in Decatur, and before long horses and cattle and donkeys and goats began finding themselves part of our family.

Ridin'

By the time I was about ten years old I discovered that I had a real knack for riding. I began breaking Shetland ponies for farmers in Wise County. For my pay I was allowed to keep the horse for several months or even a year with the owner furnishing the feed.

By the time I was thirteen I began breaking full-sized horses for cow work. As a rule, the owner of the horse would either pay me $25.00 or let me keep the horse for one year with him furnishing the feed. This assured me of plenty of good riding horses and, on the other hand, it assured the owner that he would have a well-broken horse by the end of a year.

Two Horses To Break

One day a man named Cecil Hoyle came by the house to see me. He was a tall, slender man who lived on our street. It is one of the ironies of life that when people spoke of him they did not mention the fact that he was a fine, honest, hard-working, sober citizen who was a credit to our little town. Instead, people mentioned the fact that he was the nephew of the famous gambler who wrote the book, *According to Hoyle.*

Anyway, Mr. Cecil told me that he had a young mustang stallion he wanted me to break for him. This two-year-old horse not only had wild blood flowing in his veins but had run free all of his life. He had never had a rope around his neck and, as far as Mr. Hoyle knew, had never even been close to a man. After Mr. Hoyle had explained this to me, he asked how much extra I would charge to break this wild fireball.

But by this time in my career I had begun to think of myself as quite an outstanding horseman. So when he asked if I would charge him anything extra I very modestly replied,

"Shucks, Mr. Hoyle, they all look alike to me! The wilder they are the better I like 'em! I'll break him for the same price as anything else—$25.00 to get him saddle-broke and bridle-wise, or I'll keep him a year and you furnish the feed." Mr. Hoyle said he would be delighted to furnish corn and oats for the horse and let me keep him for a year. We shook hands, and that was that.

The very next day old' Dump Dunaway came by. Dump had been a mighty good man in his day, but by now he was pretty well used up. It turned out that he, too, had a horse for me to break. It was a fine bay gelding of blooded stock. The horse was young and strong and was in the large Jones pasture about three miles out of town. But, Dump warned me, the horse was as wild as a deer—had never been touched by a rope and, as far as he knew, had not even seen a man close up.

What would I take to break him? Again I very modestly put forth the opinion that if he had a head, tail and four legs I could handle him easy!

"Shucks, Dump, they all look alike to me," I said, and we shook hands on it. He, too, wanted me to keep the horse for a year with him furnishing the feed.

Kelly

There came upon a day that Rusty Matheson, a tall, skinny friend of mine, went with me to get the mustang stallion. We were well mounted, and the seven-mile ride out of town to the Hoyle place was pleasant enough. When we arrived we rode out into a large prairie pasture where a number of horses were grazing. It was not hard to spot our horse.

He was really something to see! He would have been an outstanding horse in any herd. He was of Quarter Horse conformation, medium-size, light brown color with a buckskin face and a long, black, wavy mane and tail. He was not only beautiful but had an alertness the Arabians call "The Look of Eagles."

He stood off by himself, and we decided to cut him off from the rest of the herd and rope him. But we soon had another thought—we couldn't get close enough to shoot him, much less rope him! He not only had tremendous speed but unusual endurance. We chased him for several miles, and our horses were lathered up and breathing heavily, but the young stallion was as fresh as though he had been out picking daisies.

We went back to the band of horses and roped fresh cowponies from the herd. Quickly we changed saddles, mounted the fresh horses and renewed the chase.. Again he ran away from us without ever getting into high gear.

We chased him for several hours and finally, by pure luck, ran him into a fence corner, and I managed to throw a rope around his neck. "Now run," I yelled at him. Let him try to run across the prairie pulling me and my horse after him. That would fix him and fix him good! He could learn his first lesson right here and now.

But instead of frantically struggling against the rope and trying to run away as I expected, he came straight for me! His mouth was open, his neck outstretched, and obviously he intended to knock me off my horse and stomp the living daylights out of me.

Frankly, he scared me half to death, and I hollered for Rusty to help as I slapped him across the nose and spurred my horse out of the way. Rusty made a wild throw with his rope and, for just about the only time in his whole life, roped what he was trying to rope.

His lariat settled smoothly around the horse's neck, and he rode one way and I rode the other, holding the wild horse in the middle so he could not get at either of us.

For some reason or other, I named him Kelly on the spot.

"We'll See Who's Boss"

We had caught him, but getting him home was another matter. We were seven miles from town, and that horse fought every step of the way. In the first place, Rusty and I had to be careful to be always far enough apart that Kelly could not get at either of us. Then that crazy horse would hold back until the choking ropes would force him to come forward in order to breathe. So he would plunge forward, get a couple of gulps of fresh air, and then hold back again. The day was hot, and it sure made hard work for our horses. We had to stop again and again to give them a breather. The only trouble was, Kelly always took a breather too, and it seemed to do him more good. I thought surely his neck would be getting stiff and sore and he would soon get tired of fighting, but it just didn't work out that way. He fought every step of the way to our place.

And the more he fought, the madder I got! By the time we got home I was just about spittin' nails. That horse needed a lesson, and I was just the fellow to give it to him. Although it was getting dark, I couldn't wait until the next day to show him who was the boss at the Rice place. What's more, he would be so tired that he would be easier to ride now than after resting all night.

So we wrapped his rope around a snubbing post, and I tried to saddle him. But he was just as determined that I wasn't even going to get near him with that saddle, and he kicked, struck and fought until he finally actually choked himself down. When he fell on his side, we quickly slacked the rope so he could breathe, and I slapped a saddle on his back. As soon as he got his senses back he struggled to his feet, but while he was still dazed I cinched the saddle and, although he tried, he couldn't buck it off.

We dragged him over to a small plowed field, and while Rusty snubbed him to his saddle horn, I stepped into the saddle.

"Let him go, Rusty," I yelled. "I want this horse to find out who the boss is around here!"

He didn't find out who the boss was, though. He bucked into a ditch and fell head-over-heels with me, and it knocked my arm out of place.

It was several weeks before my arm healed enough that I could try it again. By this time Kelly was completely rested and spoiling for a fight.

Kelly The Rebel

When the day came that I rode him again, it was some battle. Most grass-fed horses do not have the stamina for prolonged bucking. But no one had ever told Kelly! Like I said, he had unusual stamina. As soon as he had his head, he ran a short distance and then "came unwound." Again and again he shot high into the air, humped his back, kicked straight up with his hind legs and landed almost standing on his head. He hit the ground so hard I thought sure it was going to burst me wide open. My nose began to bleed, and my stomach felt like it had been turned upside down and backwards!

Pound—pound—pound! Up-and-down, up-and-down, up-and-down! With each sickening jar I grew weaker. I realized if this kept up much longer I was licked.

And then, just before I fell off—Kelly gave up, stopped bucking and broke into a plain gallop. I felt like the little boy who had been to see the dentist. "Dad," he said, "the tooth came out just before it killed me!" Kelly had stopped bucking just before throwing me sky-high.

Although I was sick at my stomach and a bloody mess, I was also greatly relieved. I had won the fight, and Kelly would never try so hard to throw me again. As a rule a really wild horse will desperately wage an all-out war the first time a cowboy tries to ride him. But if the cowboy stays on, the horse will likely feel it is useless to buck so desperately a second time. It is mainly a matter of training a horse after he has been thoroughly ridden the first time.

But evidently Kelly had never read a book on breaking wild horses, and he didn't know he wasn't supposed to buck just as hard a second time! The next time I got on him he bucked furiously again. And the next time. And the next!

That horse was a natural-born rebel. He was absolutely determined that no one was going to be his boss, and this rebellious spirit characterized his entire life. Of course I learned to ride him easily enough after the first couple of times. And finally, by punishing him with quirt and spur, I broke him of bucking. But then I had to break him of kicking and biting and striking. And when he was punished so much that he decided there was no percentage in that, he changed tactics—and tried running away with me! More than once when I was helping cowboys drive a herd of cattle, he would clamp the bits in his teeth and bolt right through the entire herd and scatter cattle all over the prairie!

Wasted Ability

Kelly was a real disappointment to me. He had tremendous speed. In all my life I think I have only ridden one other horse that could run as fast. But I never knew exactly **where** he was going to run after he got started. I had to watch him every minute.

And he had tremendous endurance. Once I was supposed to help on a cattle drive but overslept. I saddled Kelly and ran him all the way to the Five-Mile Crossing to catch up with the drive, and it didn't bother him a bit.

But his rebellious spirit kept him from being the valuable horse he was qualified to be. Incidentally, I think he is the only horse I have ever handled in my life that did not like me. No matter how much I petted him or how often I brought him bread and apples and other good things to eat, I think he hated me.

I kept him not one but two years. He never did make a trustworthy horse, and when I finally sold him for Mr. Hoyle, he only brought a fraction of the price of a top cow horse.

The Other Horse

After I started the training of Kelly, I went to get the bay horse of Dump Dunaway's. He, too, was a striking horse. He was a blood-bay—beautiful red in color with heavy black mane and tail.

In size he was larger than Kelly, but he did not quite have that same alertness, that "Look of Eagles" of the fiery mustang.

Here was another horse that had never known the feel of a rope, and again Rusty and I shook out our ropes and went after a wild horse. Again it was a chase, but I was familiar with the Jones' pasture, and we soon had the bay in a corner and a rope around his neck.

Of course he reared and plunged, fought the rope and tried to get away. I let him drag the horse I was riding around the prairie for awhile until the red horse was winded. I decided to ride him then and there, and Rusty snubbed him to his horn while I slapped a saddle on his back and stepped into the saddle.

It was something strange to him, and it scared him and he bucked. He went straight across the prairie for less than one minute, going in high, springy jumps. Then he stopped, breathing hard and quivering. I gently eased up on the reins, and he began shaking his head, fighting the bits, and going in circles. Again I gave him his head, rubbed his neck, and he began to grow calm. In less than half an hour, I could step in and out of the saddle without his moving a muscle.

In an hour's time I was riding alongside Rusty as nice as you please.

By the end of the afternoon he had completely lost his fear of me and was as gentle as though he had been handled all his life. From that time on, it was just a matter of training.

Denver

I named him Denver.

During the year I had him, he gained quite a reputation for himself (and for me) around Decatur. Any number of cowboys wanted to buy him, but Mr. Dunaway was a man of his word, and he let me keep the horse a full year.

Oddly enough, Denver was not an outstanding horse as far as looks or speed or stamina were concerned. Oh, he was a beautiful horse, but he still would never have won a blue ribbon in a horse show on his beauty or build or movement.

Nor was he especially fast. Kelly could have run circles around him any day of the week.

And when it came to endurance, Denver was just an average, healthy horse with average stamina.

Yet in spite of the fact that he was very average in looks and natural ability, many a cowboy would have given his eyeteeth for Denver. When Dump finally sold him, it was for the highest price ever paid for any horse I had ever broken. And the fellow who bought him certainly got his money's worth. Of all the horses I have known in all my life I must list Denver among the really great ones.

I believe the thing that really made Denver such an outstanding cow horse was his **attitude** — his friendly disposition, his **willingness** to be used. After the first twenty or thirty seconds under a saddle he never, never tried to buck again. He never one time tried to kick anyone. Although a spirited animal, he was perfectly safe for any man or woman or child to ride.

My dad leased the Jones pasture to graze a herd of cattle and we let Denver run on his birthplace. Often we would drive out in Joe's (my late brother, Evangelist Joe B. Rice) Ford, and I would cup my hands and whistle for Denver. If he could hear me at all, he would come on a dead run, mane and tail flying in the wind. He loved to be ridden, and I often drove up cattle for my father without using either a bridle or a saddle.

Almost always he would follow the Ford back down to the gate. Sometimes I would let him follow us back to town. It was a beautiful thing to see this red horse, in a dead run, following that Ford car down the highway! I would sit in the rumble seat of that old Ford yelling, "C'mon, Fellow! and on he would come, free as a bird without rope or halter. Right through the middle of town, across the square and down west Main Street we would go with Denver galloping along behind.

Hundreds and hundreds of people saw this and marveled.

Denver loved anyone who was kind to him, and he especially loved my mother. Although she was crippled from a stroke of paralysis, Dad would help her down the kitchen steps, and she would call Denver and feed him sugar, salt, cookies, cornbread, left-over biscuits and other goodies so enjoyed by a gentle-natured cow pony.

He would always come when he was called and, oddly enough, would never leave our yard once he was home.

I had never loved a horse so much before, and I was greatly pleased when, at the end of my year, Dump sold him to a fine rancher who gave the red horse a good home.

Rebellion Or Surrender

Over the years I have thought again and again of those two horses—Kelly and Denver. And I have often marveled at the fact that the lesser horse was the greater. And I have often wondered just what kind of a horse Kelly would have been if he had not lived a life of rebellion. He was so beautiful, so speedy, so strong and so tough. With his speed he would have been wonderful for calf roping. Because of his agility he would have made a great cutting horse. With his unusual stamina he likely could have won any 100-mile endurance ride.

And yet all of this wonderful, wonderful ability was wasted because Kelly would never submit to the guidance of his master. He was filled with rebellion and hate.

On the other hand, Denver, the ordinary, became very extraordinary. Seemingly he did not possess any special gifts except—he had unusual intelligence. He knew that he would get the most out of life if he became what his master wanted him to become.

And today I find many young people who remind me of those two horses. I find young people who are talented, who are so gifted they can do almost anything. And yet they are so foolish as to be rebellious against God.

"Foolish?" Yes, for **"The Fear of the Lord is the beginning of knowledge"** (Proverbs 1:7a).

Every Christian might as well put this fact down once and for all—no one is going to get the most out of life who is rebellious against God. No matter how beautiful or handsome, no matter how witty and gay, no matter how talented and smart...the rebellious

Christian is going to find out, when it is too late to do anything about it, that he has missed the best in life as far as God, loved ones and self is concerned.

In Mark 8 Jesus said, **"For whosoever shall save his life shall lose it; but whosoever shall lose his life for my sake and the gospel's, the same shall save it."**

Does this sound like double talk? Well, it isn't. The one way for anyone to lose his soul is to try to save it his own way. And the way to save your soul is to trust Jesus with it.

And, Good Neighbor, the sure way to lose your life is to leave Christ out of the picture and try to make the most of life by yourself and in your own way. And the way to get the most out of life is to turn your life over to Christ.

All of us realize we are going to live here in the flesh just this one time. And all of us want to make the most of this one time in which we live. Why not remember, then, that Jesus came that you **"might have life and have it more abundantly."**

My good friend, I am sure that you want the very best life has to offer. I urge you to be wise enough to know that the best in life comes through surrender, through obedience to the Lord Jesus Christ.

SHEEP

A MESSAGE ON THE SHEPHERD AND SHEEP. AN INTERESTING STORY AS TOLD BY DR. BILL RICE WHEN PREACHING ABOUT THE GOOD SHEPHERD AND HIS SHEEP.

Everywhere you go in Palestine you see shepherds and sheep. Everywhere you go! The Princess (Cathy) and I were in Jerusalem for 11 weeks just resting up. I had had malaria from the jungle in Africa. One day we were up on the Mount of Olives; then we walked on down to the Garden of Gethsemane. It is about halfway down the mountain. I like the Garden of Gethsemane. They are making it smaller every year. It is being built on more and more. After staying there for a while, we finally left and walked on down the mountain. Right in front of us was the temple and the temple gate and the little Valley of Kidron. We had gotten on down to the valley and started to go up the other side. We looked, and up in front of the gate was a shepherd. He had his back to us. He had on a striped robe that came down to the calf of his legs. And he had on sandals and a keffiyeh. That is the thing they wear on their heads that hangs down their backs. The shpeherd was leaning on a staff. He had his back to us, and all around him was a flock of sheep. It was beautiful!

There was a little rock wall, and the Princess and I sat down, and I said, "Isn't that the prettiest thing? You know what? That's how David looked. Sure as shootin', that's how David looked." There was the shepherd and the robe and the staff and all that. And while we looked, suddenly we heard a noise. We looked. Here came another shepherd with a whole bunch of sheep. When these two men saw each other they spread their arms. They rushed together like freight trains and hugged and kissed.

It bothers me to see men kiss, but they hugged and they kissed and they pulled whiskers and they slapped faces. They loved each other. You often see men walking with their arms around each other. You never see a man walk with his wife in Palestine unless he is a foreigner. In these two men you could see Jonathan and David. These two fellows pulled whiskers and they slapped faces and they hugged and they kissed. And while they were doing this, the sheep got mixed up. They wandered all around, all smelling noses and talking to each other.

I said to my wife, "Great guns! When these two lover boys wake up they'll be fit to be tied."

It is a cowboy's nightmare to have two herds of cattle mixed up. It takes from now to Christmas to get two herds of cattle separated.

But while they were hugging and kissing we looked and, so help me, here came a third man with a bunch of sheep. Another shepherd. He saw the other two shepherds and said, "Salome, salome. Effendi salome." They all rushed together and all three of them began hugging and kissing and hitting faces and pulling whiskers. Another flock of sheep—they were spread out everywhere and all mixed up.

Again I said, "Man alive! Somebody ought to tell their wives they'll not be home for breakfast. These men are going to be here practically forever trying to get all the sheep separated." I sat down on a little rock wall with my wife. I just couldn't wait (this is mean I know) but I just couldn't wait for them to realize what had happened.

Finally, here came the hugging and kissing. One fellow backed up and began to leave. He then turned around to walk away.

"He doublecrossed me." I said, "Oh my, he sold his sheep. That isn't fair. I have been waiting all this time." He didn't even know yet about the sheep being all mixed up, as far as I knew.

He walked maybe as far as 30 to 40 feet. Never stopped walking. Over his shoulder he said, "Mmmmmm, brrrrrr, mmmmmm, brrrrrr."

And I never saw anything like it in my life. Sheep all over the place picked up their ears and looked and came scampering after him. He never stopped walking. He didn't stop and count them. He just kept on walking. And his sheep followed after him.

If we could teach our cows to do that, we would have it made! There he went and his sheep following him. I couldn't believe it.

Then I had to wait for the next shepherd. After a while the hugging and kissing and the whisker-pulling and the face-slapping began again. And the shepherd started walking in the same direction of the other shepherd. Over his shoulder he called, "Mmmmmm, brrrrr, mmmmm, brrrr." And here came the sheep. I never saw anything like it in my life.

We waited until just about dark. It was gloomy and dusty and at last the one shepherd who had been standing there all this time turned and walked off. As he walked, he said, "Mmmmmm, brrrrr, mmmmmm, brrrrr." And here his sheep came running after him. It was a thrilling sight to see.

After that, I had to try and get sheep to follow me. We would be in a taxi going some place and we would see a shepherd and sheep. I would tell the taxi driver, "Hold it! I want out. I want to go over there and look at those sheep." We'd go over there, then I'd say to the taxi driver, "Ask him if I can talk to his sheep."

"If you can do what?"

"Ask him if I can talk to the sheep."

The taxi driver would say something in Arabic. After getting permission, I'd walk out to the sheep. I've done this again and again.

The sheep would all be grazing. I'd walk out to them and say, "Mmmmmm, brrrrr." They wouldn't even look up. Not a nose! I'd change my voice — high, low. Nothin'! It was the beatenest thing. By that time the shepherd, of course, was in convulsions. He thought it was the funniest thing. That stupid American over there carrying on. More than once I have pulled out a piece of money and said, "Hey, you come call them." And he would walk up and say, "Mmmmmm, brrrrr," just like I did, and every sheep would come trotting up to him.

Sheep, you know, have perfect pitch.

Jesus said, 'My sheep hear my voice and they know me. They won't hear the voice of an hireling. They won't follow him.'

That is the truth. They tell me a hundred shepherds could line up, and every last one of them could go through this "Mmmmmm, brrrrr" business. But, until the sheep heard his own shepherd, he would pay no attention. The sheep would come only to the voice of their shepherd. It is an amazing thing.

Palestine today, even in this mechanized day, is still a country of sheep and shepherds.

Jesus said, 'What man of you if he had a hundred sheep and if he lost one of them, wouldn't he leave the ninety and nine? Wouldn't he go after the one that is lost? Wouldn't he look for it?'

Kamar Goes Quickly

THE BIG WHITE STALLION HAS A GOOD EDUCATION, GOOD CONFORMATION AND GOOD ANIMATION. BUT PERHAPS HIS FINEST CHARACTERISTIC IS THE FACT HE IS ALWAYS READY TO DO THE BOSS'S BIDDING ON THE DOUBLE!

We have about 85 horses here on the Ranch, and we are expecting a colt crop of about 25 more within the next few weeks. But my personal mount is a large white cow horse named Kamar the Brave.

Kamar is about 15 1/2 hands high. (A "hand" is about four inches.) And he will weigh between twelve and thirteen hundred pounds. So he is somewhat larger than the average cow pony.

Kamar started life as a grayish-brown with small spots all over his body. He is a registered Appaloosa of the "leopard" type.

(Some Appaloosas have a light blanket with dark spots on the rump, while the rest of the body is a solid color. But a leopard Appaloosa is usually of a light color with tiny dark spots peppered all over his body.)

But by the time Kamar was three years old he had turned a silvery-white with tiny, tiny little black spots from head to tail. In the winter his heavy coat completely covers these little spots and he appears to be snow-white. But in the summertime the little spots may be seen, especially around his face and neck.

A Good Education

Kamar has been well trained as a working cow horse. He will respond instantly to the slightest movement of the rider. He will start, stop and turn at the slightest touch of the rein. When driving a herd of cattle and a steer tries to make a break, he will sometimes plunge into a dead run to head him off before I even realize what that steer is up to. He has a lot of what cattlemen call "cow sense."

The first time I ever used him for work was about two years ago when he first came to the Ranch. I was driving a group of yearling colts to the corral at John Rice's farm. It was a beautiful spring day, and all of us were feeling great. The colts had broken into run, and Kamar and I came thundering across the pasture behind them. Most of the colts headed straight for the corral gate and dashed inside. But one golden two-year-old suddenly whirled and flashed out across the field toward the back pasture. Instantly Kamar whirled and was after him on a dead run. We quickly overhauled the colt, and I intended to pass him and head him back toward the corral. But when we were alongside the colt, he suddenly ploughed to a halt and then whirled and ran back to the corral.

Kamar did the very same thing! I had not realized how well trained he was, and when he whirled to follow the colt, he and I just about parted company! As I felt myself going out of the saddle, I managed to grab the horn and to hang on when he straightened out—still in a dead run—I managed to scramble back into the saddle, feeling mighty foolish as I did it.

His training shows up when I am using a rope, too. We get along great except for one thing—he thinks I am a better roper than I am. Every time I through a rope at a steer or a calf, he evidently thinks it is impossible for me to miss and immediately begins backing up! If I rope the animal, of course that is the thing for him to do—get that rope tight as quick as possible. But when I miss, it is downright embarrassing for him to begin backing across the corral dragging nothing but an empty noose!

I sure do appreciate his calmness when a steer or a horse that has been roped begins to fight. He never gets excited but simply braces himself and lets the critter fight. When I snub a wild horse up close, it may push against him or tug away, but he never fights back, doesn't even flatten his ears! And this, of course, leaves me with both hands free to handle the rope and try to subdue the fighting animal on the end of the rope.

He is calm, too, when a gun is used around or on him. It is a rare thing I ever ride here on the Ranch without slipping a six-shooter into the saddle holster. If I fire a gun unexpectedly he may jump. But if I make sure he sees me draw the gun, he will hold perfectly still while I aim at a rabbit or a squirrel or anything else.

Of course I try never to shoot over his head or to hold the gun so that the muzzle blast will hurt his ears.

No Spurs Needed

Above all, Kamar has one characteristic that any horse I am going to ride **must** have—a willingness to go at all times. I simply will not have a horse for my personal use if he must be spurred or kicked or whipped in order to make him move and move fast!

Now, if I am using a rope, I usually do wear spurs. In that way I can get the message to him faster by nudging him with my heels than I could by the pressure of my knees. But this is not a matter of laziness on his part—it is simply for efficiency.

Kamar is always ready to run!

God Loves Runners

It is in the matter of moving that so many preachers miserably fail. I have known many a preacher who has been blessed with a good mind, a radiant personality and has acquired a good education—and still isn't worth the powder it would take to blow him up! They simply are not willing to use themselves for God. The soul-winning work they do is almost incidental. They are not willing to put out that extra something that means the difference between feeling rested and feeling dog-tired. They are not willing to deny themselves food, rest, recreation or even entertainment.

But God loves Eager Beavers. God uses the fellow who is always up and at it.

My famous big brother, Dr. John R. Rice, has been referred to as "The Twentieth Century's Mightiest Pen." And I think this is a true description of him. **The Sword of the Lord** has been published in millions of copies, and it is read around the world. His books and pamphlets have gone into the millions of copies, too. And yet John Rice said a very surprising thing to me one day when we were driving home from the airport in Nashville.

We had been speaking in a conference at the First Baptist Church of Hammond, Indiana, where Dr. Jack Hyles is pastor. It was a great conference, and I was honored to have been on the program. Driving home from the airport in my car, John and I began talking about how good God had been to us in our marriages, our children and our ministries.

After a few moments' silent reflection, my brother said, "I know the Lord has certainly been good to me. And strangely enough, I have no real talent except a talent for hard work!"

Now I do not agree for one minute that John Rice does not have many and great talents. But I would agree, I think, that every talent he has is the result of downright hard work. He is a great writer, but he has not always been—he has practiced writing morning, noon and night for many, many years! I have been with him in conferences and seen him sit on the edge of his bed with a pencil and paper in his hands, writing page after page of a sermon! He is a great writer because he has really practiced and worked at it!

And even now words sometimes do not come easy to him. I one time saw him struggle for a phrasing of a ten-word telegram!

In Christian work, as a rule, great achievements are primarily the result of great effort.

God uses the person who makes himself usable and available!

In the eighth chapter of Acts we notice that Philip **ran** to carry the Gospel to the Ethiopian eunuch.

In the Parable of the Great Supper we read that the master of the house said to the servant, **"Go out quickly into the streets and lanes of the city, and bring in hither the poor, and the maimed, and halt, and the blind."**

Notice that it was urgent to reach these handicapped **quickly** with the invitation to come and dine.

And if we are going to reach the handicapped for Christ, our key word must be **"quickly."**

Not Since Adam

Isn't it strange that since the days of Adam and Eve until now there has never been a real world-wide effort to reach the handicapped for Christ! Especially the deaf.

We are really going to have to move quickly, then, if we are going to get the gospel to the deaf around the world in our generation. And yet it can be done, and if you and I will just buckle down, really mean business, really sacrifice and work and pray—It can be done in our lifetime!

Harvest fields among the deaf are ripe around the world. Good Neighbors, it is time for us to go at a gallop!

THE BIG TOE OF SAINT PETER

SOMETHING NEW WAS ADDED TO THE WORSHIP SERVICE IN THE WORLD'S LARGEST CATHOLIC CHURCH! AND IT ALL HAPPENED BECAUSE OF AN EVANGELIST WITH AN INQUISITIVE MIND AND AN ITCHING NOSE! CATHOLICS AND PROTESTANTS HAVE ONE WICKED THING IN COMMON IN SO-CALLED WORSHIP SERVICES—AND THIS SIN IS SYMBOLIZED BY SAINT PETE'S BIG TOE!

EDITOR'S NOTE: 1979 will go down in history as the year the Pope visited America. While great crowds rejoiced at the sight of this powerful leader, this editor was saddened by the error of Romanism the Pope represents. Not only does this man advocate salvation by works, he encourages a "formalism" which becomes more important than truth, and sadly, many, including Catholics and Protestants, follow after his teachings.

During the recent Sword Tour, we were in Rome, Italy. The Princess and I had been there before, and we were looking forward to seeing this historic city again.

Of course everyone who visits Rome wants to see the Basilica of St. Peter in the Vatican City. This is the largest "Christian" church in all the world. It is 610 feet long and the ceiling is 150 feet above the floor. Of course the great dome, designed by Michelangelo, is much higher.

It is not only the largest "Christian" church in all the world, but is surely one of the most beautiful. Viewed from the outside, it is an imposing church. The great dome is covered with gold leaf, and it shines in the sunshine like a ball of fire. I have flown over Rome in an airplane, and it has always been easy to spot this beautiful golden dome.

And it is beautiful on the inside. Of course—like so many Catholic and Protestant churches in Europe—it does not resemble a church at all on the inside. There are no seats, no pews for a congregation. It is more like a great art museum with statues and paintings around the room. The floor is of beautiful marble tile. In various niches around the wall there are altars where priests say Mass. Bodies of various popes and saints have been buried in the walls and in the floor. And, speaking of bodies, you can see several bodies of popes in glass caskets scattered here and there about the room!

The Statue Of Saint Peter

But the most interesting thing in the entire building to me is the statue of Saint Peter. It is made, I suppose, of bronze. At any rate, it is made of metal, and it has turned black. It is not a great big statue, but is probably about twice life-size.

Peter, with curly hair and short beard and mustache and wild-looking eyes, is seated in a chair. He is dressed in robes. His right hand is raised about shoulder high with the trigger finger pointing up toward Heaven. His left arm is in a sling for some reason or other, but he is holding a giant key in his left hand. He is wearing sandals on his feet, and there is a halo above his head.

The statue rests on a marble pedestal that is about 4 1/2 or 5 feet high.

His Right Big Toe

About the first thing you notice about the statue is that part of his right foot is missing. The big toe has been worn away until most of the first joint is gone. There is no toenail—just a round, shiny stub. And it doesn't take long to find out what happened to the big toe on his right foot.

It has been kissed away!

People stand in line to come by and kiss Saint Peter's big toe. Most of them first wipe the big toe off with a handkerchief or the sleeve of a coat or dress. And the reason is not hard to discover. Some people just aren't very dainty kissers.

I saw one fat, bald-headed fellow walk up to Peter's toe, cross himself and then begin kissing. He did a thorough and prolonged job of it.

Kiss ... kiss ... smack ... pop ... suck ... slurp ... slobber ... squish ... kiss ... gurgle ... smack ....

When he had finished kissing, he again crossed himself and then repeatedly rubbed his hand over the toe and then rubbed his hand all over his face and then the toe and then his face.

His Other Toe And My Itching Nose

The 43 members of our party had gathered around the statue, and we were watching and waiting for an opportunity to examine the statue more closely. I had stepped in line and walked up to get a close look at Saint Peter's right foot. Then I looked at the left foot that is further back from the edge of the pedestal and is out of kissing range. I noticed that the toe of the left foot was not at all smooth and shiny like the toe of the right foot. Moreover, the big toe on the left foot was a great deal longer. As I looked I wondered just how much of the right toe had been kissed away through the years. Taking a ball-point pen from my pocket, I measured the length of the left big toe. It was about four inches long. As I turned to measure the right big toe, my nose began to itch, and I paused long enough to give it a couple of brisk rubs. Then I measured the right toe and found that approximately 1 1/2 inches had been kissed away.

I then stepped aside for the next fellow, and it was then I realized something new had been added to this toe-kissing business. The next fellow happened to be a fairly short man with a large bay window. He stood on tiptoe and strained to reach over and rub Saint Peter's left big toe! He then kissed his hand and crossed himself as he turned to kiss Saint Pete's right toe! This little fellow had been standing behind me. Evidently he had not noticed the ball-point pen in my hand, and when I had measured the left toe and then rubbed my itching nose, he thought I had rubbed the toe and was then kissing my hand!

So he had done what he had thought he had seen me do.

I was a little perplexed at this, but I was downright startled at what happened afterward.

Every person in the line that followed did exactly the same thing!

One by one they came by, rubbing Peter's left toe and kissed their hand and then went on to kiss the right toe! Some of them were tall like I am, and they had no difficulty in reaching the left toe. But others were short and fat, and they had to strain and grunt to rub that left toe! But rub it they did! Each one had seen the preceding person do it, and that was the way it ought to be done.

I stepped back by the side of John Rice, and he and I watched this "follow-the-leader" business in amazement. And in sorrow for these poor people, who were going through a ritual that would not help them to know God but rather would keep them from Jesus Christ and salvation.

Going Through The Motions

This business of just going through the motions, of a pat ceremony—is always wrong. I do not say it is always insincere. I just say it is always wrong.

For all I know, the prophets of Baal may have been sincere on Mount Carmel when they cut themselves with knives and howled and danced and prayed to Baal. But whether they were sincere or not, it is certain they were dead-wrong.

It is just as wrong for a Catholic to call on Simon Peter. He could neither forgive sins nor answer prayers even when he was alive. He certainly cannot do it now. Much less a statue of the Great Disciple. Furthermore, to kiss the toe of the statue can be nothing less than idolatry. In Exodus 20:4 and 5 Almighty God says,

"Thou shalt not make unto thee any graven image, or any likeness of any thing that is in heaven above, or that is in the earth beneath, or that is in the water under the earth: Thou shalt not bow down thyself to them, nor serve them: for I the LORD thy God am a jealous God, visiting the iniquity of the fathers upon the children unto the third and fourth generation of them that hate me."

And if this unscriptural ritual is wrong for the Catholics, then it is just as wrong for Protestants.

Formal Worship Centers

As all of us know, modernism is a great threat to the church of Christ today. But, Good Neighbor, I have never in my life heard of any sound, fundamental church going modern until it has first become stiff and formal. Formalism leads to coldness. As our churches become more formal in appearance, more formal in procedure they become more dead spiritually and more open to modernism.

During a revival campaign in a large Baptist church in Minnesota, I was invited to speak to the young people on Sunday evening before the main service. I was ushered into a small auditorium. On the platform there was a table. On this table there were brass candlesticks and a brass cross about 2 feet tall. When everyone was seated two young men lighted the candles and the other lights in the auditorium were turned off. Then, at a pre-arranged signal, several young people led in prayer while the organist played classical music! When I was introduced to speak the leader explained that this was their "Worship Center" and they only wanted enough light to "see the cross." He went on to say that he hoped I would be able to speak without reading any Scripture since they did not want any light turned on to break the "spirit" of the meeting! Great guns! As I headed for the light switches I half expected someone to grab a rosary and begin, "Holy Mary, Mother of God, pray...."

It is becoming a fairly common practice in many churches to have such a cross and candlesticks—and perhaps a picture of Christ—prominently displayed on the platform. And they are often considered objects that are especially holy and sacred.

The So-Called "Worship Service"

And the so-called "Worship Services" are surely an abomination to God. I am utterly amazed at all the pastors who otherwise seem to have ordinary good sense and yet who go in for these cut-and-dried, stiff, formal, dull and deadening "Worship Services."

The music, of course, consists of old hymns sung very slowly. (Many people believe that dullness and reverence are the same thing.) Usually no song leader is used. There is no life, no joy in the singing. Organ music predominates.

As a matter of fact, the organist often ramrods the entire service. The organ toots and the choir marches in. The organ toots and the choir is seated. The organ toots and the choir sings "Glory

Be to the Father." The organ toots again and the congregation stands to sing the Doxology!

The choir will sing—or attempt to sing—an anthem. The smaller the choir, the more high-falutin' the anthem they shriek, falter, and stutter through! Reminds me of a little boy with a painted-on mustache and a mouth organ trying to look and sound like Sousa's entire band!

And the "pastoral prayer"! Man alive—how fancy can you get! The preacher thanks God for sunshine and flowers and that Old Glory still waves from the flag pole. He will not only quote Scripture in the prayer but will give the references so that the Lord can go and look them up for Himself if He doesn't believe they are really in the Bible! Often this must all be in King James' English double-plus.

Now, it's all right with me if a preacher wants to use **"thee"** and **"thou"** and **"thine."** I hardly ever do it myself but I see nothing wrong in it. Even an occasional **"hast"** may be in good form and good taste. But deliver me from the stuffed shirt who puts an **est** on every other word in his prayer. I don't see why he doesn't go whole hog and pray in Latin.

And let me frankly say that I suspect the good judgment of any preacher who prays to music. Does anyone honestly believe that God is more likely to listen if our prayers are accompanied by music on the organ or piano? Of course not. The music is for its effect on the congregation—not for its effect on the Lord. It seems to me that this borders on irreverence and hypocrisy.

Formality in preaching, in praying and in singing—all of this leads to carnality rather than spirituality. Churches that are truly reverent, that build up the saints and win the lost are churches of joy and fire, of energy and zeal—churches that are **alive!**

Let me say again that I have never known a church to embrace modernism that did not first embrace formal "Worship Services."

Empty Honour

Had Jesus been standing with us that day in Saint Peter's, watching people kiss the big toe of the statue, I think He might again have said,

"This people draweth nigh unto me with their mouth, and honoureth me with their lips; but their heart is far from me."—Matthew 15:8.

And if Jesus were to visit some of our churches that have cold, formal, ritualistic services, that simply go through the motions of worship—I think very likely He would say the same thing to them.

Homecoming!

TEDDY NOT ONLY GOT THE GIRL, THE WEALTH, PRESTIGE AND FAME, BUT HE ALSO GOT THE ACCLAIM OF THE OLD HOME TOWN WHEN HE AND JIM CAME HOME.

Jim and Ted were both the kind of a fellow that is usually used as the hero in a novel. Both were born and raised in a medium-size, middle-western town. Both of fine homes, both had parents whose financial standing was a little better than average, and both boys were endowed with fine minds and bodies. Their families were close friends, and both boys were pals from the time they were little boys learning to walk.

In college, as in high school, both were outstanding. Of course they were roommates, and each was still the other's best friend. Fraternities and societies welcomed them with open arms. As in high school they were extremely popular with the faculty as well as the student body. Everyone recognized that these were "up-and-coming young fellers."

The first three years of college life passed quickly and happily. They made top grades, and extracurricular activities were gay and exciting.

Near the beginning of the fourth year, however, two other people came into the lives of Ted and Jim who where to have lasting influence upon them for the rest of their days. First was beautiful, vivacious Jane. From a prominent family, she was quite a person in her own right. As the old-timers used to say, she was "fair of face and form." Sunbeams danced in her hair and mischief in her eyes. Although she had been born with a silver spoon in her mouth, she was sweet and unspoiled—a campus belle any university would be proud to claim. And both Jim and Ted fell madly in love with her.

The second person to have a lifelong influence on the boys—at least upon Jim—was an evangelist. This man of God had come to the city for a revival campaign, and many of the young people attending the university went to hear him. Some went out of curiosity, others for entertainment, and others because they felt the evangelist might be able to point them to something or Someone Who would fill a lack in their lives. One evening, when an invitation was given, Jim quietly left his seat and walked forward to openly confess the Lord Jesus Christ as his own personal Saviour.

His entire life was changed! II Corinthians 5:17 says:

"Therefore if any man be in Christ, he is a new creature; old things are passed away; behold, all things are become new."

The parties and social events that had taken so much of his time and filled so much of his life now seemed so empty and tasteless. There was an admiring, worshipful love for Jesus in his heart that he had never dreamed possible before. He was so overwhelmed with his own salvation that he told everyone about it with whom he came in contact. Night after night he invited classmates to go with him to the revival meeting, and more than once he walked down the aisle with some chum he had led to Christ.

His dreams for the future changed, too. He no longer dreamed of being a lawyer or statesman. In his heart he heard the Lord asking, **"Who will go for Me?"** and he, like the prophet of old, answered, **"Here am I, send me."**

He determined to serve the Lord. But how? and where? At first he was rather surprised when he felt a definite impression that he ought to go to the then mysterious land of Africa. With his skill as a public speaker, he rather marveled that God did not want him to do the work of a pastor or an evangelist. But day by day as he prayed and waited on God, he became more and more convinced that the Lord was leading him to the Belgian Congo.

The youth began to realize more and more what he would face should he go to Africa. He began to realize more and more what he must leave behind here in America.

And Jane—what about Jane! She, too, had turned to Christ. Although he had not yet asked her to marry him, she knew he loved her and had indicated that his love was returned. And yet...if he went to Africa he must leave Jane behind. He could not ask a woman he loved to share the unknown dangers, privations, sicknesses and hardships that would await him there. If he went, he would have to leave her behind. Could he bear to live without her?

Again and again he searched his own heart and life and motives. He spent many long hours in tearful prayer and meditation. He felt he ought to go to Africa—and yet he felt he simply could not give Jane up. Finally, he made his decision. He had spent the preceding night in prayer—had not even gone to bed. During the morning hours he had not gone to classes but has stayed in his room to pray. Shortly before noon, he stood before his window and looked down upon the magnificent campus.

Suddenly it seemed to Jim that Someone else was standing beside him. Jesus was standing beside him, looking through the open window. He seemed to feel a strong, warm, friendly hand—a beautiful hand with an ugly scar—placed on his shoulder. It seemed to him that Jesus quietly said, "I know the struggle you are going through. You see, I, too, had to face a great decision. I, too, left the ones I loved to minister to others."

Tears filled the young man's eyes. After all Jesus had done for him, could he do less than give himself completely to the Saviour? Moreover, Jesus Himself had promised, **"And everyone that hath forsaken houses, or brethren, or sisters, or father, or mother, or wife, or children, or lands, for my name's sake, shall receive an hundredfold, and shall inherit everlasting life."**

"I'll go, Lord Jesus," Jim whispered.

...That evening he told Jane. As they walked among the trees on the moonlit campus, he told her of his call, of the need of taking the Gospel to those who had never heard. When she placed her hand on his arm and protested that many here needed his ministry too, he simply said, "I guess God wants me to love those who are not loved by anyone else. He wants me to care for those who have been neglected so long. There is no doubt in the world but that He wants me in Africa, and so I feel I must go."

They stood looking at one another for a few moments in the moonlight, and the he said gently, "Goodnight, Jane, and goodbye. Pray for me, Dear, as God lays it on your heart."

Silently they parted, never to meet again in this life.

...Up until this point the lives of Jim and Ted had been so much alike. Now they could hardly have been more different. After a time of careful preparation Jim sailed for the Dark Continent. He was one of the first white men to penetrate into the Congo. He was one of the first missionaries ever to spend his life there. In a small hut with a thatched roof he studied hour after hour, day after day, week after week, to learn the native language. Here he gradually made friends with the natives. Little by little he won the confidence and then friendship of the people. Time and again he walked many weary miles through jungle paths to minister to some sick man or woman or child. Again and again he sat in the shade of a mud hut to carefully explain the Gospel of Christ to these lost people who had never heard of God nor Christ nor the Bible. Seldom did he ever see another white person to whom he could talk. Rarely did he receive mail from home because it took months for a letter from the states to reach the heart of darkest Africa.

Year in and year out Jim studied, prayed, preached and lived Christ. God blessed his efforts. He became known as a friend to the black man. Souls were saved, lives were changed, savage customs forsaken through the ministry of this godly **Jesus-talker**. Down jungle trails, over rocky mountains and across broad prairies, Jim's fame spread until he was known to millions of African natives. Dozens, then hundreds, then thousands of them made their way to visit the Jesus **Bwana**. A village sprang up around his mud hut, and day by day he preached Christ to the multitudes.

But this work took an awesome toll in the missionary's health. Malaria had ravaged his body from the first month he had set foot on African soil. He suffered the fever, from splitting headaches and nausea and dysentery. Other tropical diseases had found him, too—jungle fever and dread belhartzia and typhoid. His body had suffered from external causes. His strength had been sapped by countless scorpion stings. A misdirected arrow from one of his own beloved converts had torn his left eye completely from the socket and left him one-eyed. A mother leopard attacked him, and before she was driven off had crushed the bone in his right leg just above the ankle, and he walked with a painful limp to the end of his days.

Before 20 years had passed, Jim was already an old, old man. With white hair, deeply lined face, sightless left eye, thin, sick, a cripple and desperately tired.

...Runners burst excitedly into Jim's village one morning with startling news—a safari led by several white men was making its way toward the camp. Of course Jim was excited. This meant news from home, men with whom he could speak in English, perhaps a few books and even letters from friends back in the States. Never in the world, though, did he dream what this safari really had to bring him—it brought him Teddy! Yes, utterly unbelievable as it seemed, Teddy was at the head of the group.

The years had been kind to him. He had known virtually every success that any man could desire. He had won Jane for his wife—and a lovely, loyal wife to him she was. He had won fame as a wise and brave young officer during the Spanish-American War. It seemed he was always at the right place at the right time and did the right thing. Finally he had actually been elected President of the United States and served two terms in that capacity. He was now in robust middle life with a wonderful wife, splendid children, wealth and fame. Having a great love for sports, he had decided to visit Africa on a hunting expedition, and it was only natural that he should look up his old friend while he was there.

There was a doctor in Teddy's party, and when Teddy suggested that he should give Jim a thorough physical check-up, Jim agreed. With kind frankness the doctor told Jim that he had not long to live. If he ever expected to see America again, he must go back when Teddy returned to the States. His days were definitely numbered. The hard work, hot climate, jungle diseases, malnutrition and physical hardships had so impaired his health that he was an old, worn-out sick man, while Teddy was still fairly young and in robust health.

...Early one morning several months later, the train pulled in at the station of the old home town. The long trek out of the interior to the coast of Africa, and then the long ocean voyage home, had been almost more than Jim was able to bear. When his ship arrived at New York City he had written the pastor of his home church, telling that he had returned to the States and was on his way back home. The jolting, dusty train ride of several days' duration had taxed his strength to the utmost. Jim painfully stepped down from the train, expecting to see many of his old friends there to greet him. He felt sure the pastor and the head of the missionary organization and many of the old friends would be on hand to welcome him home. Imagine his disappointment, then, when he did not see a single familiar face. Some who had come to the depot to welcome arriving friends looked curiously at the thin, one-eyed man with white hair as he limped painfully to find a telephone inside the depot.

Jim called the parsonage, only to find that the pastor was not in. Jim talked to the pastor's wife. Yes, they had received his letter. No, she had not heard the pastor mention whether or not they had expected him to speak in the church and tell about his experiences on the foreign field. She was sorry but they had not arranged a place for him to stay. He could just make his own arrangements and go to any hotel or lodging place he chose. He could contact the pastor later on in the day if he would like to do so. She was sorry she could not talk to him longer, but the Ladies' Aid was having a luncheon in the church, and she must hurry to prepare for it!

Dazed, Jim turned away from the phone and limped to the street where he engaged a taxi carriage. He hardly knew where to go or what to do. He had expected, of course, that the church would provide a place for him to stay. He thought they would want to have him speak and tell about the wonderful opportunity of winning the unsaved in Africa to Christ. But it seemed no one was very excited about his return home after so many, many years on the foreign field. He had very little money and knew he could not afford a hotel. The carriage driver directed him to a small rooming house in the slum section of the city, and there he engaged a small, dirty, dark room in the attic.

For a couple of hours the frail, exhausted man sat on the edge of a narrow cot with his head in his hands. He was so tired and so heartsick and so discouraged and so bewildered. For a long time he sat there, wearily wondering what to do next.

Suddenly he became aware of the sound of music. It became louder and stronger until he could distinctly hear—far away—the playing of a band and the voices of a great multitude of people. As he listened, the music became louder and the sounds more distinct. Suddenly it dawned on him that the music was coming closer. He pulled himself up from the cot and limped to the window. Peering with his one eye through the little window, Jim was utterly amazed to see a parade marching down the street straight for his little rooming house! The hometown band was playing a rousing air as it marched at the head of the procession. Cheering crowds thronged the sides of the street. A long procession of horse-drawn carriages followed the band.

On the procession came—straight down the street toward the dying man who watched from the attic window. His heart beat exultantly. It was a surprise welcome home! They had not forgotten, after all. No wonder there had been no one to meet him at the station. This was why the pastor had not answered the phone. Now he understood why the pastor's wife had been so vague and seemingly unconcerned. They were giving him a surprise welcome home—such a welcome as he had never dreamed of. They would ask him to speak, and again he would tell a multitude of the grace of God who sent His Son into the world to die for sinners. He would tell them of Africa and its dying millions and plead for their prayers and support.

But as the parade drew nearer he saw an open carriage drawn by milk-white horses. In the carriage there stood a man who was waving his tall silk hat to the wildly cheering crowd.

It was Teddy! Teddy, too, had come back to the old home town, and the city had turned out to welcome him. Teddy had been away on a hunting trip, and the newspapers were filled with his exploits, and they could hardly wait to give him a hero's welcome home. In the parade were the town dignitaries: the mayor, the councilmen and the prominent pastors. No doubt Jim's own pastor was in the procession.

As Jim stood in the darkened little room and peered through the dirty window, his heart was filled with bitterness. It was not fair. He had given up everything for Christ—Teddy had taken everything for himself. He had given up his family and friends and the girl he loved. He had lived a life of poverty and sacrifice in the midst of danger and disease. He had carried the gospel message to those who had never heard. He had lived a life that was clean and holy that men might believe what he had to say about the Son of God. Teddy had married the most wonderful girl in the world, had achieved wealth and fame; had had everything a man could wish for. Jim had been gone for years and years, and on his return home there had not been a single person to meet him at the depot; not one single family had asked him to their home for even a meal; his own pastor had not even arranged for him to speak in the old home church. Teddy had been gone a few months, and yet had been given a hero's welcome on his return home.

It simply was not fair! It was not right! He had given everything for Christ, and no one cared. Teddy had taken everything for himself and was given a royal homecoming welcome by the people who had heaped every honor upon him. It simply was not right, was not fair.

Suddenly Jim sensed the presence of Someone else standing beside him in the darkened room. He realized that Someone else was looking through the little window at the cheering crowd on the street below. It seemed that a strong arm was placed across his thin shoulders, and again he felt the touch of the nail-scarred hand. He felt a strange sweet peace fill his troubled heart as he and his Lord stood side by side gazing through the little window. At last the Saviour spoke.

"Yes, it is fair, my brother," Jesus said. "This man has lived for the world, and it is only fair that the world should reward him. He has lived for the world, and you must not feel badly because the people of the world have given him such a splendid welcome on his return home."

The nail-scarred hand tightened on the dying missionary's shoulder.

"My brother," Jesus said, "you are not yet home! You have not lived for the world, and you must not expect to be rewarded by the world. You have given your life for me, and your labor has not been in vain, your work will not go unrewarded. Your citizenship is in Heaven, and it will not be long before you will be going to your heavenly home. Wait until you see the welcome we are planning for you, at your home-coming! But you are not yet home!"

Good neighbor, each of us ought to decide whether we will live for this present world or for eternity. The Bible says, **"...he that cometh to God must believe that he is and that he is a rewarder of them that diligently seek him."** Do we believe that? If we do, then we ought to live like it. We ought to live sacrificially. We ought to do something that is good and noble and sacrificial with our lives.

THE ATHEIST IN BUGHOUSE SQUARE

One of the most unique city parks in all the world must surely be Bughouse Square in Chicago. Sightseeing buses make regular stops there and thousands of people have gone back to homes all over America to tell of what they have seen and heard at this public park.

Actually, Bughouse Square is a lovely little park about one mile north of Chicago's Loop. The grass is green, there is a lovely little fountain, there are rosebushes and, of course, benches where anyone who wishes may stop and rest. It is located just a few blocks from Moody Bible Institute.

There is nothing unusual about the looks of this little park. It is what goes on there that is so unusual. Bughouse Square, you see, is a speaking place for absolutely anyone who has anything he wants to say.

I have heard of preachers of all sizes, shapes, colors and denominations speak from an improvised platform in Bughouse Square. I have heard Communists speak there. I have heard atheists speak there. In a single afternoon there may be twenty speakers in rapid succession. One man may tell why he thinks the American flag should have more (or less) stripes or why he feels the stars should be in the middle of the flag or perhaps in a border around the flag. The next man may tell why he is against putting grass in public parks! He may insist that it takes too much money to water the grass and to mow it and it is an absolute shameful waste of the taxpayers' money! The man who follows may declare we should reduce our armed forces and the next man may make a speech insisting that the color of policemen's uniforms should be changed from blue to purple! I have heard men tell why they believe in prohibition, others tell why they did not believe in prohibition. I have heard advocates of free love. In fact, I have heard men speak on just about every subject imaginable. Decent things and indecent things, men who used the most eloquent language imaginable and men who spoke with a steady stream of profanity and obscenity.

Of course you may wonder why I spent so much time in Bughouse Square. Well, I actually did not spend a great deal of time there. But when I was a student at Moody Bible Institute I at one time had a job taking visitors sightseeing around Chicago and visitors always wanted to see Bughouse Square. So, again and again, I left visitors standing in the crowd or sitting in the car listening to the speakers while I passed out gospel tracts among the audience.

I am just sorry I was not present when the following true story took place.

The Atheist

One day an atheist was among the speakers. This was not uncommon at all but this man was an uncommonly good platform speaker. Evidently he had read the works of Bob Ingersoll and had memorized many of his phrases and had copied many of his arguments. And on this particular day he was really going great guns. He declared he knew there was no God and before he had finished speaking there would not be a man in the entire audience who still believed there was a God. He knew there was no God, he said, because some people got rich and others were poor. This just was not fair and if there was a God, He would never allow it. He went on to discuss sickness and poor health and oppression and old age.

At the conclusion of his speech he said, "Now ladies and gentlemen, I am going to prove to you conclusively that there is no God. It will just take me one minute to do it."

With that he pulled a silver watch from his vest pocket, held it in his left hand and dramatically raised his right hand toward the sky. As he looked toward the heavens he shook his fist upward and thundered, "God, are You up there? If You are I have something to say to You. I hate You. You are not fair! You are not just! You are mean! You are a bully! You ought to go to Hell! I hate your guts and I always will! Furthermore, I promise You I'll never change! I'll hate you till the day I die."

"Now, God," he continued, "since I hate You and am trying to get everyone else to hate You—why don't You kill me? If that pack of lies called the Bible is true then it would be easy for You to do. But I dare You to do it. I ask You to do it. I beg You to do it. I defy You to do it. I'll give You exactly one minute in which to kill me and if You don't kill me in that minute I will know and all these people will know it is because there is no God!"

The atheist then solemnly held the big silver watch in view of the people. Five seconds passed. Ten seconds. The people were shocked and stunned. Not one person in the entire crowd said a single word. It was as though the hush of death were on the audience. When thirty seconds had gone by the atheist again shook his fist as he yelled up at the sky, "Better hurry up, God. Get a move on. Thirty seconds has already gone by. People are losing their faith. They'll never believe in You again. If You expect anyone in this crowd to ever believe in You again You'd better hurry up and kill me quick."

Although many in the congregation lived wicked and corrupt lives, they were shocked by this blatant blasphemy. Forty-five seconds passed—fifty seconds, fifty-five and then sixty. The atheist said nothing for a moment but looked at the crowd with a cynical smile on his face. Calmly he put his watch back in the vest pocket as he looked from face to face. What he had said and done was dramatic and, to many, convincing. Finally he spoke.

"Ladies and gentlemen," he said, "there is no such person as a Heavenly Father. There is no God. I don't believe there is one person in this whole crowd who can ever again believe there is actually a God. If there is any person in this entire crowd who believes there is still a God in Heaven, I just wish you would step forward and give us one good reason for still thinking so."

The Moody Student

The atheist was as surprised as the audience when a young fellow who may not have been over nineteen years of age, walked forward. The young man stepped up beside the atheist and said,

"Sir, I certainly still believe there is a God in Heaven and I believe I can give these people a good, logical, common-sense reason why God didn't kill you a while ago."

The atheist stepped back. He clearly felt the young man was going to make a fool of himself and he, for one, was going to enjoy it. With a mock bow he said, "Go right ahead, young man, you have the platform."

The young man faced the crowd. Everyone wondered what in the world this young man was going to say in answer to such a dramatic demonstration as they had just witnessed. But the young man did not seem the least bit uneasy and he did not keep them in doubt very long as to what he would say.

In a calm voice he said, "Ladies and gentlemen, I am a student in the Moody Bible Institute. I go to the Loop room each noon and work a couple of hours. Just a little while ago I finished my work and started walking back toward the Institute. I decided to come here and pass out some tracts before going back to school.

"A few minutes ago I was walking down the sidewalk a very strange thing happened to me. A little boy eight or nine years old suddenly stepped out of an alley and confronted me. He was dressed in rags, he was filthy with dirt and his tousled hair looked like it had never been combed. He stepped right in front of me and held out his hands to stop me.

"Where do you think you are going?" he asked me belligerently.

"I told him I was going back to my room at Moody Institute. I looked at his dirty face, his gaunt cheeks, his hollow eyes and his ragged clothes.

"Is there anything I can do for you?" I asked.

"None of your blank business," he snarled back. Then he added, "I hate guys like you with your white shirts and your shiny shoes! You are just a big bully! Do you wanna fight?"

"No, I don't want to fight," I told him, "I would like to be your friend. Wouldn't you like to have me get you something to eat and perhaps a haircut and some clean clothes?"

"Ignoring my offer of friendship the little fellow spit on me and yelled at the top of his voice, "You're scared to fight! You're afraid!

You're bigger than I am but you're scared of me. C'mon put up your fists!" And with this he called me a number of vile and filthy names.

"I tried to walk around him but he jumped quickly in front of me shaking his fists up in my face and daring me to fight.

"I didn't fight him. With the palm of my hand I could have slapped him halfway across the street, of course. He was such a small fellow. But I would not have hit him for the world. My heart went out to him in pity. I would gladly have bought him some food, would have given him a bath and some clean clothes. I would like to have been a big brother to him. But he wouldn't let me. The friendlier I talked to him the more foul-mouthed and vehement he became.

"Finally, with a heavy heart, I stepped around him and walked on down the street. For a block he followed at my heels daring me to stop and fight and calling me every sort of a vile name.

Two of a Kind

"Imagine my amazement, ladies and gentlemen," the young man continued, "when I came here and saw the entire incident acted out all over again. Back up the street a dirty little boy with an evil mind and wicked words ignored my offer to feed and clothe and cleanse him. He insisted on calling me wicked names and daring me to fight. Then I walked down here to the park and find a dirty little man shaking his fist in the face of God and defying God to kill him!

"A dirty little boy and a dirty man—two of a kind!

"He wants someone to tell him why God did not strike him dead. It was for the very same reason that I did not strike that dirty little boy up the street who kept on daring me to fight.—I felt sorry for the little boy and wanted to help him. God feels sorry for this man and wants to help him.

(By this time the atheist had stepped off the little platform and had lost himself in the crowd.)

"The little boy was filthy with dirt and I would gladly have given him a bath. This man is filthy with sin and needs to be washed in the blood of Jesus Christ.

"The little boy was dressed in rags and I wanted to get him some nice, clean clothes. This man is dressed in rags, too. They are the rags of his own self-righteousness. He would like you to believe he is so righteous and honest when he is really filled with pride and arrogance and deceit. He needs to be clothed in a robe of righteousness that only the Lord Jesus Christ can give.

"And the little boy was hungry. He did not say so but I knew that he was. He looked pale beneath the dirt, and undernourished. I would gladly have fed him but he had nothing but abuse for my offer of kindness. And this man, too, is hungry. His heart is hungry. Something is missing and instead of being happy he is bitter. Jesus, who is the Bread and Water of Life would satisfy him completely but instead of being grateful for God's offer of salvation, instead of thanking the Heavenly Father he has nothing to offer but abuse and cursing.

"Yes, ladies and gentlemen, I can tell you why God did not strike him dead. It is because God loves even a man like this! The Bible says, *"For God so loved the world, that he gave his only begotten Son, that whosoever believeth in him should not perish, but have everlasting life."* (John 3:16).

"And God has patiently waited for this man to be saved. The Bible says, *"The Lord is not slack concerning his promise, as some men count slackness; but is longsuffering to us-ward, not willing that any should perish, but that all should come to repentance."* (II Peter 3:9).

"Certainly, God could easily have killed this man while he held his watch in his hand. But what's the rush? God is still giving this man an opportunity to be saved. If he persists in refusing the Lord Jesus Christ, then in due time, he will die. The Bible says, *"And as it is appointed unto men once to die, but after this the judgment:"* (Hebrews 9:27).

"So if this man will not turn to Christ he will die all too soon—and after that he will be in Hell forever.

"But he does not need to die without Jesus Christ. And I want to invite him here and now to turn to Christ, confess his sins, and be saved."

But when the young man looked around, the atheist was nowhere to be seen. With his head bowed he had long since made his way through the crowd and had quietly left the park.

"Ladies and gentlemen," the young man continued, "I have some gospel tracts and I would like to give one to each of you. Please remember that God loves you and will save you even today before you leave this place if you accept the Lord Jesus Christ as your Saviour."

With that the young man left the little platform and passed out the gospel tracts among the crowd. I understand that many a man had to wipe tears from his eyes before he could read and I wonder if many a person did not turn to Jesus Christ that day in Bughouse Square.

I SAT WHERE THEY SAT

IN UNUSUAL WAYS GOD PREPARES HIS SERVANTS FOR THEIR OWN PARTICULAR FIELD OF SERVICE. OFTEN GOD PUTS US IN THE OTHER FELLOW'S BOOTS THAT WE MAY APPRECIATE HIS FEELINGS AND HIS NEEDS.

The Israelites were in captivity. The Lord selected Ezekiel to minister to them. To prepare Ezekiel for this ministry God not only told him about the Jews but placed him among them for seven days. Ezekiel 3:14 and 15 says in part, *"So the spirit lifted me up, and took me away...Then I came to them of the captivity at Telabib, that dwelt by the river of Chebar, and I sat where they sat, and remained there astonished among them seven days."*

The the Lord went on to explain to Ezekiel that he was to be a watchman to warn the Jews of their sins and to try to get them to repent and turn to their God.

My own heart has been greatly stirred as I have read the words. *"I sat where they sat."* Ezekiel became one with these broken-hearted men in captivity. If he was to minister to them it was important that he should know their hearts and lives.

Put Yourself in the Other Fellow's Boots

Empathy is one of the greatest words in our language. Not **sympathy** but **empathy**. It means putting yourself in the other fellow's needs, his longings, his joys and his sufferings.

God wanted Ezekiel to minister to those who were in captivity, so He placed Ezekiel in the midst of them. **Ezekiel sat where they sat.**

Jesus Became One of Us

When the Saviour came to the earth to minister to mankind, He became a man. In Philippians 2:5-8 we read,

"Let this mind be in you, which was also in Christ Jesus: Who, being in the form of God, thought it not robbery to be equal with God: But made himself of no reputation, and took upon him the form of a servant, and was made in the likeness

of men: And being found in fashion as a man, he humbled himself, and became obedient unto death, even the death of the cross."

Jesus put Himself in our boots. He became one of us. He knew what it was to be hungry, to be alone, to be betrayed and to suffer persecution and death. He put Himself in our place. That is why Hebrews 4:15 is such a wonderful verse, and it is the cause of encouragement in Hebrews 4:16. Let me quote the two verses—

"For we have not an high priest which cannot be touched with the feeling of our infirmities; but was in all points tempted like as we are, yet without sin. Let us therefore come boldly unto the throne of grace, that we may obtain mercy, and find grace to help in time of need."

Jesus not only has sympathy for us but empathy. He knows just exactly how we feel and what we need.

And God has used many a converted convict to reach other prisoners for Christ because He knows their needs so well. He sat where they sat!

And God has used many a converted down-and-outer to establish rescue missions that have turned many a vagrant, many a drifter to Christ. Again—because he sat where they sat.

Will You Sit Where the Deaf Sit?

And today God needs those who can understand and will help the deaf. For the last two weeks we have had scores of deaf teenagers here on the Ranch. It was the largest group of deaf teenagers that has ever gathered here on the Ranch for gospel services.

And it was the largest group of deaf teenagers ever to gather any place in all the history of all the world in a camp for gospel services!

And it was a fairly representative group. There were beautiful girls and some not so beautiful. There were handsome boys and some not quite so handsome. There were boys and girls with brilliant minds and some not quite as intelligent. There were some happy and well-adjusted and some with problems of which the average person has never even dreamed.

But all of them are human beings, all of them are people and all of them have problems and needs that someone must help them with.

All Handicapped

Just to be deaf is a very serious handicap. In the nature of the case it means they are barred from many spiritual, educational, recreational and social advantages that are open to those of us who can hear.

Many of them never go to church because they have no idea in the world what the sermon, songs or Sunday School lesson is about. They can't even meet people without being embarrassed when they cannot speak their own name or understand the other fellow when he tells who he is.

It is difficult for them to play with hearing children who usually have neither the patience nor the ability to get along with the deaf.

Socially, of course, they are left out of almost everything.

The deaf must live in a little world of their own—unless—God puts some of us among them. Unless the Lord causes us to sit where they sit. Unless the Holy Spirit puts it into our hearts to try to understand them and to help them.

Bill Rice Is No Ezekiel

Ezekiel said, *"I sat where they sat."*

I am no Ezekiel. I have never been deaf. I have never been one of them.

And, yet, in some sense, I can say that I sat where they sat.

I know what it is to be lonesome, to be left out of everything, to be "that skinny little fellow in patches." I know what it is to be ridiculed by my classmates, to be the butt of cruel jokes.

I know what it is to be unwanted, to be without a home, without parents, without friends. I know what it is to be hungry. I know what it is to sleep in haystacks and under bridges and in barns. I know what it is to wear patched clothing and to be too poor to buy either a hamburger or a haircut!

So my heart goes out to the fellow who is handicapped, who has had nothing but bad breaks, who can't fit in with others—the boy or girl who is a misfit whether it is his fault or not.

Since Cathy and I have been married we have known what it is to be very, very poor. We sure do know our neighbor's turnip patch furnished a large portion of our food. We ate turnips boiled, baked, french fried and mashed; we ate turnip soup and turnip sandwiches!

We worked our way through Moody Bible Institute in Chicago where we lived in a tiny, dark basement apartment most of the time. For the first year we spent about as much time prowling back alleys looking for bottles we could sell or fighting rats, mice, cockroaches and bedbugs as we did in the classroom!

When we first moved here on the Ranch we lived for six months in a small, open-air cabin with no furniture except beds and two chairs and a one-burner electric hot plate.

So the Princess and I know what it is to be poor and alone. Our hearts go out to these wonderful deaf youngsters who need our help, our love and our understanding so badly.

The Doubly Handicapped

But these who are deaf often have other handicaps, too. Sometimes the same accident or sickness that causes one to be deaf will cause him to be almost blind or to be deformed in some way or other.

We had a number of wonderful young people with us just this summer who are doubly handicapped. In fact, our own ward had a double handicap. He had endured operation after operation because of a harelip and cleft palate. Even the deaf shunned and ridiculed him. At first he was keenly hurt. Then he became angry and sullen. Then he had begun to get mean and vindictive when he came to camp and was saved. He has become a wonderful fellow, and we love him and are proud of him and thank God he belongs to us. But there are others like him who need someone to care and to help.

Others are dwarfed or have twisted limbs or have suffered polio or muscular dystrophy. All of these are in need of someone who will sit where they sit, who will try to understand and will try to help.

The Harvest Is White

The Lord Jesus reminds us that the harvest is white and He asks that we pray for more laborers. Good Neighbor, as I have said time and time and time again, workers are needed among the deaf.

Desperately needed.

Won't you please try to put yourself in the place of a deaf boy or girl? Won't you please realize their need of someone to love them, to guide them, to befriend them and—to win them to Christ.

If you would only take the trouble to learn Sign Language—and it isn't hard—there's no telling how many deaf young people you could influence for good and for God.

And many others of you ought to sacrificially support the work we are trying to do. We are honestly trying to serve God in the winning of the deaf for Christ.

I urge you to sit where they sit. And I remind you that surely your reward will be great in Heaven.

"Excuse Me From Heaven!"

THE BOY WHO "FELL" OFF HIS DONKEY—AND LANDED IN A TREE! EXCUSES FROM A GUILTY CONSCIENCE ARE SILLY, FOOLISH AND DAMNING!

Rusty and I were riding our donkeys down the road that led to the little western town of Decatur, Texas. We lived there. It was a hot summer afternoon. We had been to Sandy Creek for a swim and now we were trying to get back home in time for supper.

As we rode along on the slow-moving little donkeys our heads and feet were bare, our hearts were light and we were two happy little boys except for one thing—we sure were hungry.

On the left of the road was the farm of an old fellow named Hiram Keye. Mr. Keye was a deacon in the First Baptist Church and, as far as I know, a fine old fellow. He never seemed to smile and was never friendly to us youngsters and so we put him down as an old grouch.

Anyway, just past the house was a large peach orchard. The road went over a small hill and, on looking back, Rusty and I discovered that we could not be seen from the house. By mutual consent we turned the donkeys in the orchard gate and rode up among the trees to "borrow" some large and luscious peaches.

I rode beneath a tree and quickly pulled four or five peaches, stuffed them into my pockets and was ready to go.

"C'm on, Rusty, let's go," I said.

"I ain't ready yet," Rusty replied.

I had already turned ole Buck toward the gate but I stopped and looked back over my shoulder to see what was causin' the delay. To my surprise I saw Rusty standing up on the back of his donkey and stuffing peaches into his shirt. He was wearing overalls but was also wearing a belt around his waist and the peaches would go inside the shirt and fall to the belt and stop there. He had already stuffed so many peaches inside his shirt that he looked like a skinny little boy with a big roll of fat around his belly!

"Rusty! You cut that out!" I yelled at him. "I don't really think Mr. Keye would care for us getting a few peaches to eat but what you're doing is just plain stealin'."

"Who cares," he indignantly replied, "I never did like old man Keye anyway and I'm gonna get all the peaches I want."

"Well," I said, "you'd better c'mon right now or you're gonna git into...."

I was going to say "trouble" but I didn't say it—I saw it! Just a few feet away, beneath a peach tree, I could see just the legs of a man walking stealthily around the tree toward Rusty. I gave old Buck a slap on his rump to get out of there. When Buck started Rusty's donkey followed and Rusty, taken by surprise, yelled, "Hey!" and grabbed hold of the limb above his head.

The man jumped from behind the tree and yelled, "Bill, stay where you are!" And, believe, me, I "stayed."

It was old man Keye, himself. He looked up at Rusty hangin' from the limb, his shirt full of peaches and his face so white that the freckles stood out like stars on a flag.

"Donald," Mr. Keye thundered up at Rusty, "what are you doing in that tree?"

I will never, never forget Rusty's historic reply. In a thin, squeaky voice he finally managed to say, "I just fell off my donkey!"

I don't know what kind of an answer Mr. Keye expected—that is if he expected any at all—but he certainly hadn't expected **that**. He looked at poor Rusty incredulously. Then he grinned and then he howled with laughter. I bet it's the first time that old man had laughed in fifty years. He sounded like rusty nails being pulled out of a tin roof. At first he doubled over and walked around in circles. Then he became so weak he began to stagger. Finally, he sat down and fell over on his side screeching and howling with laughter. Tears ran down his face like sweat dropping from a horse's flanks.

All this time I was watching the old farmer with my mouth open while sitting on my donkey. Poor Rusty, watching in horror, was desperately hanging up in the tree. It was plain he was too scared to turn loose and too tired to hold on much longer.

Finally the old fellow motioned Rusty to drop and then left me to hold the donkeys while he and Rusty went up to empty the peaches around Rusty's middle into Mrs. Keye's dishpan.

Guilty Excuses Always Silly

I have enjoyed many a chuckle over that time Rusty "fell" off his donkey and landed in the peach tree. Of all the stupid, silly answers! And yet I have found, through these wonderful years as an evangelist, that most guilty excuses are so stupid, so foolish, so silly that only an idiot could believe them. Just ask any man why he isn't a Christian and the chances are many to one that he will lie to you. He won't say, "I'm not saved because I don't want to be saved." Not on your life! He will answer with some excuse that is so silly and foolish that even a little child would know he is lying.

Hypocrites in the Church

I wonder how many hundreds of times someone has said to me, "Dr. Bill, I am not a Christian because there are so many hypocrites in the church. Now I am just too honest to be a hypocrite and I am not willing to associate with those who are."

Yet that very same fellow will work at a factory or farm or railroad yard with those very same hypocrites he is not willing to associate with in church! Although he does not want his children in Sunday school with the children of the hypocrites, he sends them to the same public schools! Moreover he and the hypocrites trade at the same stores, drive the same kind of cars, wear the same kind of clothes, belong to the same clubs and vote for the same candidates!

Isn't it strange that a hypocrite never bothers an unsaved man until he needs an excuse to explain why he has wickedly rejected the Lord Jesus Christ!

The honest truth is—an unsaved man is an unsaved man because he is not willing to turn from his sins and to live for Christ.

Because he feels guilty he tries to soothe his conscience and placate his friends with a stupid, silly, lying excuse that will damn his own soul and add to his torment in Hell.

The Bible plainly says, *"So then every one of us shall give account of himself to God."* **(Romans 14:12).** Men do not go to Hell because of the sins of hypocrites but because of their own sins.

Parents Forced Church on Him

During a revival campaign in a New York town the pastor and I went to call on a successful farmer. He made no pretense of being a Christian man and had never been known to go to church. When I invited him to attend the revival services he said,

"Well, I'll tell you how it is, preacher. When I was a boy my parents made me go to church all the time. I resented them making me go and got so sick of church that I decided I would never go again after I was grown and my own boss."

I looked him straight in the eye, grinned just a bit and then replied,

"All right, now tell me the real reason you won't come to hear me preach."

Although I had grinned a little and tried to speak pleasantly, it got under his hide and made him mad.

"You mean you think I'm lying?"

"I know you're lying," I said, "and don't get sore until I tell you how I know you're lying. When you were a boy there were many things your parents made you do that you did not like. They made you take baths and comb your hair. They made you wash up before you came to the table to eat. They made you go to school. They made you work.

"Now that you are a grown man and your own boss you still do these things. You still work and you still study—that is proven by the fact that you are a successful farmer. You still take baths and you probably take more now than you did then because you know it is healthy and right. When you were a boy you didn't have enough sense to know what was good for you and so your parents had to see to it that you did right. But when you became a man both your parents and God expected you to have enough sense to do right without someone making you. The Bible says, *'When I was a child, I spake as a child, I understood as a child, I thought as a child: but when I became a man, I put away childish things.'* (I Corinthians 13:11).

"Your trouble is not what your parents made you do when you were a boy. Your trouble is that you have a wicked heart and what you need to do is—."

"Hold it, hold it, hold it!" he said. "One sermon a day from you may be all I can take and since I'm going to be in church tonight I don't want to hear a sermon this morning! What time does church start anyway?"

He did come that night, and the next night, and the next night. What's more he had enough sense to realize he had been lying to himself all these years and in repentance he turned to Christ and trusted Him for salvation!

Feeling

Sometimes people claim they are unsaved because they do not **feel** like being saved. Perhaps he believes he must be overcome by some great emotion that will literally drive him to salvation. In the meantime, though, he is waiting for that **feeling**.

Isn't it strange that he uses far better judgment in many matters that are not nearly so important as the salvation of his eternal soul.

For example, what man **feels** like putting some of his money in the bank every week? Wouldn't he enjoy spending the money? Of course he would but common sense tells him he had better save some of his money while he can.

Does any man **feel** like climbing up on top of his house in freezing weather to put out a fire in the roof? Certainly not—but a man will do that just the same because common sense tells him he ought to save the house from burning while he can.

And, Good Neighbor, you had better realize that both your body and your soul are facing eternal destruction and if you have a lick of common sense you'd better attend to your salvation while you can.

I believe in **feeling**. I believe a sick man ought to feel better **after** he has taken the medicine and is on the road to recovery. And I believe a man ought to feel saved **after** he has been cleansed of his sins and saved through faith in Christ.

Salvation is based on **believing**, not **feeling**, and feeling always follows believing. I Peter 1:8, *"Whom having not seen, ye love; in whom, though now ye see him not, yet believing, ye rejoice with joy unspeakable and full of glory:"*

The Truth of the Matter

The real truth of the matter is, men are either saved or lost because of deliberate choice. If you are saved it is because you want to be saved. If you are unsaved it is because you want to be unsaved.

You are not unsaved because of the hypocrites in the church.

You are not unsaved because of **feeling**.

You are not unsaved because you can't understand the Bible. (Have you ever gone to a fundamental preacher and asked him to explain the way of salvation to you? He could do it in just a few minutes.)

You are not unsaved because you are afraid you can't "hold out."

No sir! You are unsaved because you are not willing to turn from your sins and accept Christ. Jesus said, *"And ye will not come to me, that ye might have life."* **(John 5:40).**

Men are lost because they **will not** accept Christ. Jesus also said, *"He that is not with me is against me..."* **(Matthew 12:30a).**

Either you are **with** Jesus Christ because you want Him to save you from your sins, to help you to follow Him, or you are **against** Jesus Christ because you are not willing to turn from your sins, you hate Jesus because of who He is and what He stands for and you are unwilling to turn from your sins to be saved.

Face It!

If you are not willing to turn to Christ for salvation, why lie about it? Why make wicked, foolish, silly excuses? Why not simply say, "I am unsaved because I prefer it that way. I love my sins and am not willing to give them up even for Jesus Christ and Heaven!"

Better yet, why not come to your sense and realize you face an eternity that will be Hell without Jesus Christ. Trust Him right now to forgive your sins and save your soul. Regardless of what you have done, God will save you before you even put this paper down if you will turn from your sins and trust Him for salvation. *"The Lord is not slack concerning his promise, as some men count slackness; but is longsuffering to us-ward, not willing that any should perish, but that all should come to repentance."* — II Peter 3:9.

BOSSY AND THE BIBLE

THE LORD USES A COW'S EATING HABITS TO TEACH US A LESSON ON PROSPERITY THROUGH USE OF THE HOLY SCRIPTURES.

As a boy in Texas I have watched many an old cow lying in the shade of a mesquite tree and chewing her cud. More than once I have leaned back in the saddle, hooked a knee around the saddle horn and just sat there watching old bossy chew. Again and again I tried to figure out what she was chewing and where she got it. I knew, of course, she was chewing her "cud" but I did not know what on earth it was or where it came from.

I know now that she is simply eating the food she has picked up earlier in the day. Unlike many other animals, a cow is not actually eating when she is grazing. When she grazes she is just storing food away which she will prepare and eat later.

Kinda Like a Cook

A cow operates kinda like a cook. When a cook goes to the store, he does not go there to eat. He goes there to lay in a supply of food he will prepare and eat later. So he gets a bag of beans, a slab of salt pork, a sack of potatoes, corn meal for johnny-cake, flour, a case of canned milk, several packages of dried apples and a bucket of sorghum molasses. He does not prepare and eat these things in the store. He takes them to the ranch to fix supper for the hands.

That evening after the day's work is done the cowboys unsaddle, feed and water their horses. Then they wash up and mosey on along toward the kitchen door. And when Cookie yells, "Come and get it," they sure don't keep him waiting! The beans with thick slabs of salt pork have been simmering all afternoon in plenty of juice. The mashed spuds, the fried apple pies, the large platters of crisp, crunchy, brown, fried corn cakes, the large tin mugs of coffee with canned milk—there is nothing better!

"B'lieve I'll try another plate of beans."

"Got any more cawn bread?"

"How 'bout some more cawfee?"

"Travel that pie down this way agin, will yu."

After the meal is over a puncher will rub his hand over his tummy and sigh, "I'll tell a man the grub is real tasty around here. If I had et any more, even my spurs wouldn't fit me."

Bossy's Eating Habits

Just like the cook goes to the store, Bossy goes to the pasture to lay in a supply of grub. She usually goes in the morning when it is nice and cool and the grazing is good. She simply **gathers** the food she will enjoy **eating** later on in the day.

A cow, you see, has four stomachs! One of them for storage of food before it is eaten. So she gathers a mouthful of grass here, a bunch of clover there. This good food she stores away. When she feels she has a sufficient supply she will probably amble off to the creek for a nice drink of water. (The water, incidentally, is carefully sidetracked into another stomach, it is not mixed with the food she has been gathering.)

To eat her meal, Bossy will carefully select a comfortable spot in the shade, lie down and begin to eat.

She regurgitates a portion of the recently gathered food into her mouth and begins to chew. AHHH—it's delicious! She looks delightedly from side to side as she chews, swallows, belches more food into her mouth, chews and swallows again. Properly speaking, she is ruminating.

Wow, this is really living!

You can almost hear her say, "Wow, this clover is good! Believe I'll have another helping of that nice grass, too!"

And so she eats the food she has gathered earlier. This time when she swallows it the food goes to another stomach where it is digested.

Chewing the Scriptures

In the First Psalm we read that in order to be "blessed" a man should not walk in the counsel of the ungodly, nor stand in the way of sinners, nor sit in the seat of the scornful. Rather, we read in verse two and three,

"But his delight is in the law of the LORD; and in his law doth he meditate day and night.

"And he shall be like a tree planted by the rivers of water, that bringeth forth his fruit in his season; his leaf also shall not wither; and whatsoever he doeth shall prosper."

The word **"meditate"** is the same as our old friend **"ruminate"** or chewing the cud.

We are to "**meditate**" in the Scriptures day and night—all the time. I cannot **read** the Bible all of the time. I cannot read while I sleep or while I drive my car or while I am riding on the Ranch. But there are times when I can read. Then while I am doing these other things I can **meditate**, I can **recall** the things I have read and think about them. Time and time again I have found strength and courage and guidance and comfort in dark hours by meditating on Scriptures I had already gathered at an earlier time.

"I'll Kill You!"

When I had been preaching but a short while I angered a wicked man by preaching on the Seventh Commandment. This man was known as a bully and had been in several shooting scrapes. He was a dangerous man to cross. When I preached on adultery he came to see me, showed me a Colt .38 in his coat pocket and asked me how I would like "a bellyful of hot lead." He said he would kill me if I crossed him again and I knew good and well I was going to have to cross him.

Frankly, I was scared. I believe in predestination, you understand, but I just don't want to put any strains on it!

About that time my sister, Mrs. Nutting, wrote me a letter and quoted Hebrews 13:5b & 6,

"...For he hath said, I will never leave thee, nor forsake thee."

"So that we may boldly say, The Lord is my helper, and I will not fear what man shall do unto me."

Neighbor, I really meditated on that Scripture. In fact, I almost chewed it to death! And I began to believe it. I lost my fear. When the bully actually walked down the aisle of the church where I was preaching, pulled that gun and yelled he was going to kill me, I stood my ground. I unnerved him so that he hesitated and that hesitation cost him his opportunity for he was soon unarmed. Later the District Attorney tried to give me a permit to carry a gun and I refused it. The D.A.'s own brother had been shot by the bully and he tried to impress on me the fact that the bully would shoot me, too.

But I continued to meditate upon the Scripture and things turned out so wonderfully it would not sound real read in a paperback novel.

Read the Bible

Read the Bible. You cannot possibly recall to your mind something you never knew! So read it! Read it and then think about it.

When sorrow comes into your life, read John 14. Then think about it. Mull it over in your mind. God will comfort your heart as you meditate on this wonderful passage of Scripture.

When you are discouraged, read Romans 8:28-39. Meditate upon what you have read. You might try Isaiah 40, also.

If you are given to worrying, read and meditate upon Matthew 6:19-34.

When you feel lonely and scared about the future try the Twenty-third Psalm. Chew on it. This Psalm has helped multiplied thousands and God will speak to your heart through it, also.

The Bible has the answer to all your questions, the solutions to all your problems. God has promised that men who live in and by the Bible will prosper in all that they do.

Someone has written,

"The Bible Contains:

"The mind of God, the state of man, the way of salvation, the doom of sinners, and the happiness of believers. Its doctrines are holy, its precepts are binding, its histories are true, and its decisions are unchangeable. Read it to be wise, believe it to be safe, and practice it to be holy. It contains light to direct you, food to support you, and comfort to cheer you. It is the traveler's map, the pilgrim's staff, the pilot's compass, the soldier's sword, and the Christian's charter. Here Paradise is restored, Heaven opened, and the gates of Hell disclosed. CHRIST is its Grand Subject, our good its design, and the glory of God its end. It should fill the memory, rule the heart, and guide the feet. Read it slowly, frequently, and prayerfully. It is a mine of wealth, a paradise of glory, judgment, and will be remembered forever. It involves the highest responsibility, rewards the greatest labor, and condemns all who trifle with its holy contents."

"All scripture is given by inspiration of God, and is profitable for doctrine, for reproof, for correction, for instruction in righteousness:" — **II Timothy 3:16.**

"Thanks" Be To God

Last night I asked my lovely wife what **unspeakable** meant. She thought for a moment and then said, "It's something that you can experience but you simply do not know how to describe."

That's right. There are many things that practically all of us have experienced but we simply do not know how to describe it to someone else. For example, how would you describe the taste of salt to someone who had never tasted salt in all his life? Or how would you describe purple to a child who had been blind from birth? How would you describe Ellis Zehr's bass voice to a little boy who has been deaf from birth?

Now multiplied millions of people have experienced the taste of salt, have seen purple, have heard music, and yet these common things are "unspeakable."

And millions of people have received God's wonderful gift, the gift of salvation through His Son, the Lord Jesus Christ.

John 3:16 tells of this gift—***"For God so loved the world, that He gave his only begotten Son, that whosoever believeth in him should not perish, but have everlasting life."***

Romans 6:23 also tells us what this gift is—***" For the wages of sin is death; but the gift of God is eternal life through Jesus Christ our Lord."***

Again in Ephesians 2:8 and 9 we read that salvation through Christ is God's gift to us.

"For by grace are ye saved through faith; and that not of yourselves: it is the gift of God:"

"Not of works, lest any man should boast."

Thanksgiving Time

Although I am an evangelist and speak to thousands of others about God's gift, I am always at a loss for words to describe what it means to be a Christian. This gift is, indeed, **unspeakable**. But I thank God with all my heart for salvation through our Lord Jesus Christ.

This is Thanksgiving time. I will not be at home. I will not have the privilege of eating a Thanksgiving dinner with my loved ones or have fellowship with the others at the Ranch. Probably some thoughtful Christians will invite me to eat with them or I will eat my meal in some restaurant. And doubtless I will spend a good part of the day and night dictating answers to letters, working on sermons, etc.

But, just the same, I expect to have a wonderful Thanksgiving Day. I know I'll be preaching once and I imagine I'll be speaking several times. It will be my privilege to tell others of God's unspeakable Gift, the Lord Jesus Christ.

And, Good Neighbor, the next best thing to having Christ as your Saviour is to share His Gospel with others.

Jerusalem's Beggar

One day Cathy and I walked through Saint Stephen's Gate in old Jerusalem. A beggar sat in the gate. He looked dirty and unkempt. His shirt was made of a striped cloth that looked like mattress ticking. A black robe covered the upper part of his body. A dirty white bandage covered one-half of a dirty, unshaven face.

He held up his hands imploringly to us and we stopped. I spoke but he did not understand English. Ahiz, the Arab Legionnaire whom the king had appointed to guide and interpret for us, had walked on through the gate out of earshot. I tried to talk to the beggar but he did not understand English. He held up his hands imploringly and said, "Baksheesh" (gift) again and again.

I took his picture, gave him a coin, and we walked on. But he was in my thoughts as I went. I wondered if he was a fake or really in need. Would the coin I had given him really be of much help? It could feed him for two or three days but he would then be in real need again.

That's the trouble with gifts that we give. We never know how much real good it will do and it will not last very long.

How different is God's **unspeakable** Gift. Jesus told the woman at the well He would give her water and she would never thirst again. Salvation lasts forever!

Thanksgiving Through Us

II Corinthians 9 is a chapter on giving. We are told we are to give cheerfully and bountifully. Verse 11 tells us that our generous giving can cause others to give thanksgiving to God. *"Being enriched in every thing to all bountifulness, which causeth through us thanksgiving to God."*

Last week I was in a revival campaign in Winston-Salem, N.C. with Paul Raker and the Faith Baptist Tabernacle. Several pastors in town asked that Mrs. Rice come and help them plan Sunday school classes for the deaf in their churches. They do not have anyone who can speak in Sign Language, etc. So Cathy spent the last weekend with me.

I announced that she was going to be there and would interpret my closing messages to any deaf who would come. Cathy came on Friday night and to our joy a good number of deaf came that same night, knowing that she would be there to interpret my message.

A strange things happened when Cathy and I walked in the door of the church. As soon as Cathy walked in, a gray-haired woman threw her arms around my wife, hugged her and smiled and cried at the same time. The woman's back was to me and in Sign Language I asked Cathy if she knew who the woman was! Cathy shook her head no. But in a few minutes we found out. The woman was deaf and after she had finished hugging my wife she began talking—in Sign Language—a blue streak! I had been in that same church five years ago and Cathy had been there to interpret my sermons for the deaf and this woman had been one of the converts.

She thanked both of us again and again and again. Cathy said to her, "It's wonderful to be saved isn't it?"

In Sign Language the lady replied, "Salvation is so good I don't know how to say it!"

That's it—it is unspeakable!

Good Neighbor, at this Thanksgiving time won't you please help others to be thankful because of your generous help in getting the Gospel to them. We are honestly trying and trying hard to please the Lord and serve Him. We are honestly trying to prayerfully use our best judgment in reaching neglected deaf youngsters for Christ. We ask you in Jesus' name that you work with us, pray for us and give with us generously.

GIFT FOR A BALD-HEADED GIANT

THE STORY OF A CANADIAN WHO FOUND, TO HIS SURPRISE, THAT HE WAS ON GOD'S CHRISTMAS LIST AFTER ALL!

Several years ago I was invited to speak twice daily on a radio broadcast in Edmonton, Alberta, Canada. During a Canadian holiday I had been asked by a group of preachers to be the principal speaker at a giant gospel rally. The program committee had arranged for two speakers in the morning followed by a picnic dinner in the open air. Then at two o'clock there was to be a thirty-minute devotional speaker followed by my message at two-thirty.

Because of the morning broadcast I could not be there until about two-o'clock. When I arrived at the weather-beaten old auditorium in the fairground, I was delighted to find that every seat on the main floor and the large balcony was packed and jammed for the afternoon service.

My singer and I were escorted to our seats on the platform. The chairman of the program committee introduced a local pastor who would, he said, bring a brief devotional message. Then after the service there would be a great song service followed by my message.

The Long-winded Preacher

It didn't turn out that way, however. The devotional speaker was having the time of his life. He was speaking to a large congregation and it was his opportunity to rise and shine! He spoke for thirty minutes. Then he spoke for thirty minutes more. It was now three o'clock. The speaker talked on. It was almost three-thirty when he finished.

Although the song service that followed was brief, it still took time to make announcements, take the offering and make the usual introduction. It was getting on toward four o'clock when I finally stepped to the pulpit. I made no attempt to bring any regular message but quoted Romans 6:23—***"For the wages of sin is death; but the gift of God is eternal life through Jesus Christ our Lord."***—and urged any unsaved to turn to Christ. I said I'd be glad to explain salvation to anyone after the service and added that if anyone left the building and went to Hell, it would be his own fault.

This was how I met a bald-headed giant of a man. He looked as mad as a wet hen and it turned out he was madder than he looked!

"Look-ee here," he yelled, shaking one ham-like hand under my sensitive nose, "you ought not talk like you do! You ain't got no right a-hurting folks' feelings like you done today!"

I retreated a step and asked, "What did I say that hurt your feelings?"

He advanced a step and replied, "You said if anybody left this building unsaved, it was his own fault. Well, I'm going to leave here unsaved, but it ain't my fault. I'm going to Hell, and I can't help it!"

"You can help it," I replied hotly. "If you go to Hell, it will be your fault. You can be saved the same as anyone else."

"No, I can't. God has predestined some to go to Heaven and some to go to Hell, and He has got me booked for Hell!"

"What makes you think God won't save you?" I asked.

"Because I have tried to get religion a couple of times, and it won't work for me. God just don't want to save me," he replied.

I told him it was wicked to talk that way about God, that he could be saved just the same as anyone else if he was willing to turn from his sins and receive Christ. I spoke so strongly, he became angry again. He asked me if I would back up my statements by actions—would I be willing to stay in the tabernacle and deal with him until he got saved, no matter how long it took. I told him if he was honest in wanting to be saved, I certainly would.

He ambled over to the edge of the platform and yelled to a woman sitting in a Ford car with some children. "Hey Ma!" he yelled, "let the kids git outta the car and go play. When you git hungry, go to the store and buy something. We ain't going home right now."

"But Pa," she said, "it's milking time."

"Forget about the cows—I ain't going to milk tonight," he said, "I'm attending to important business!"

He came back where I was and pulled two chairs up, facing each other. I thought one was for him and one for me, but I had another "think a-coming." He sat down in one and put his enormous feet up in the other, reached over to untie his shoelaces and then leaned back comfortably, looked me square in the eye and said, "All right, if you know so much, let's see you git me saved!"

For several moments I was speechless! I just looked up at him. Finally I drew up a chair and said, "First, let me show you that you are a sinner."

"Great guns," he said, "I know I'm a sinner. Get me saved!"

I turned to John 3:16. He said he already knew it by heart, but I persuaded him to read it with me again carefully. *"For God so loved the world*—did that mean him?

"Yep."

"That he gave his only begotten Son—that meant Jesus; *that whosoever*—we agreed that *"whosoever"* meant us both— *"believeth"*—and I showed him that to believe in Christ meant to receive Christ according to John 1:12—and on we went through the verse.

Then I came back to the part that says, *"he gave his only begotten Son."*

"Look, man," I said, "God gave Jesus to you long ago. You are accusing God of not being willing to save you when He has already given Jesus to you that you might be saved. Now, tell me the honest truth—have you ever taken this wonderful Gift that God offers you? Have you taken Jesus? God gave Him to you—have you received Him?"

Now it was his time to be speechless. He slowly and thoughtfully said, "Let me see that verse again." He took the Bible and looked at it long and searchingly. Then without a word from me or to me, he took his feet out of the opposite chair, went down on his knees with his elbows where his feet had been and began to weep! His great body shook, and when he could finally talk, he said, "O God, what a fool I have been! Here I have been telling folks how mean You were to me when you gave Jesus to me before I was even born and have been waiting all this time for me to take Him. I do want Him, Lord God, and I will take Him right now."

When he was finished praying, he stood to his feet. I was going to counsel with him a bit but without saying a word, he shoved me to one side and ran out of the building. "Hey Ma! Git the kids in the car. Let's hurry home and git the milking done and come back for the evening service!" It was not until later that he came to thank me for showing him the wondrous Gift of God that brings salvation.

Have You Accepted the Gift?

I am dictating this from my motel room in Newport News, Virginia. I am conducting a revival campaign here. Downtown the buildings glisten with Christmas decorations. Wreaths of holly line the streets. Store windows are filled with Christmas gifts. Every TV and radio commercial's theme is to suggest gifts for Christmas. Newspaper ads are full of Christmas bargains.

It is Christmas, Christmas, Christmas—do this, do that, go here and go there for Christmas.

On every hand people are saying, "Oh, if I could only have **that** for Christmas!"

Strangely enough, however, there will be thousands and thousands of Americans who will pass up the most wonderful gift anyone could ever get for Christmas. The gift of salvation through our Lord Jesus Christ. All other gifts get old and lose either their usefulness or their desirability. Only salvation through the Lord Jesus Christ will last forever.

With all the sincerity of my heart, I remind you that you are on God's Christmas list! Wonderful, glorious eternal salvation has been purchased for you. This is exactly what you need and it will never grow old. It will never be less valuable. It will never cease to be desirable. It will never become useless.

It is so wonderful that all the money in the world could not buy it. It is so unique that nothing else in all the world can take its place. And, Good Neighbor, the Lord Jesus Christ has purchased this gift for you.

I urge you to accept this wonderful gift. In your heart turn to Christ and trust Him to save you and forgive you of your sins. By all means receive God's Gift and have salvation for Christmas this year and all the years to follow throughout eternity.

THE HEAVENLY OMNI

THE NIGHT WAS DARK, THE MOUNTAINS THREATENING AND THE PILOTS WERE LOST—YET THEY NEED NOT HAVE DIED. AT THEIR FINGERTIPS WAS AN INSTRUMENT TO POINT OUT THE WAY.

The associate pastor and I sat across the room from the young sailor who had invited us into his home. Dr. Bob Gray, pastor of Trinity Baptist Church in Jacksonville, had given us the young man's name and expressed the desire that we visit him. Dr. Gray, himself, had called on the young man previously but had found him uninterested in receiving Christ. Now, we had talked with the young fellow for some time, and although he had been very courteous, we simply hadn't gotten to first base as far as winning him to Christ was concerned. In another few minutes, we would me leaving.

"Mr. Burris," I said, "I understand that you are stationed here in Jacksonville because you are in the Navy. Just what do you do for Uncle Sam?"

He replied that he was in the air arm of the Navy and that he was a radio technician. He worked on direction-finding instruments in airplanes. He maintained such equipment as omnis, ADF's, DME's etc. Since I own and fly an airplane, I am familiar with this navigational equipment and know its worth to the pilot.

"Before we leave," I said, "let me tell you a story that I know will be of interest to you." I then told him the following story.

Death on a Dark Mountain

Some years ago I was in a revival campaign in Pennsylvania. One black night an airplane crashed on the side of a mountain just a few miles from the church where I was preaching. It turned out that two men had taken off from the airport in Binghamton, New York and were on their way back home to Wilkes Barre, Pennsylvania. Neither of the two men were experienced airplane pilots, neither had ever flown before at night and neither was familiar with the country over which they were flying. Although they had an aerial map, the night was so dark they could not see any of the landmarks on the ground below.

Our revival service was just ending when the plane, flying low, circled the little town several times. We peered anxiously into the dark sky above, realizing that some pilot up there was probably lost. He had seen the lights of the little town below and was circling, trying to decide just where he was. After circling several times he flew off into the darkness and, to our horror, crashed on the wooded mountainside.

The pastor and I drove out to the scene of the crash. Already police cars had begun to arrive, and highway patrolmen and other police officers were sealing off the area. I identified myself and was asked to go with several of the officers to the downed plane. Most policemen realize that a preacher often comes in handy at the scene of an accident.

It turned out, however, that the plane had dived into the ground and the two men had been killed instantly. With flashlights we located their bodies, indescribably broken and burst, and rolled them up in rubber sheets.

After the bodies of the two men had been taken away in an ambulance, I walked back with a couple of the officers to examine the wreckage of the plane.

Inexcusably Lost

I was especially interested in knowing what equipment the plane had carried and when we found the battered cockpit, I borrowed a flashlight and crawled inside. As I had supposed, many of the instruments had been jarred from the panel. Even so, I soon saw that the plane had been well equipped. It not only carried a full panel including gyro compass, artificial horizon and two-way radio, but an expensive up-to-date omni!

(Of course, the man to whom I was telling this story was familiar with this instrument. In case you are not, however, let me tell you something about it. The omni is the greatest boon available to private pilots for navigation. I have two of them in my own plane. Scattered all over this nation are omni stations for the benefit of commercial and private pilots. On a cross-country flight the pilot simply flies from one omni station to another until he reaches his destination. He tunes in an omni station and the instrument in the cockpit tells the pilot if he is going toward or away from, or to the right or the the left, or directly toward the omni station!)

In the light of the flashlight, I examined the omni in the instrument panel of the twisted plane. With such a precise instrument at hand, I wondered why in the world the pilot had lost his way. Wilkes Barre, after all, was only another 15 minutes away and the omni station there could easily have been picked up on the dial. While an officer held the flashlight, I reached for the switch on the instrument and made a really startling discovery—the omni had not been turned on! Although it was within arms reach of the pilot, he had not been using it!

He had been lost...without excuse!

You've Got to Land Sometime

As I crawled back out of the broken cockpit, I pondered the death of the two fliers. It seemed to me they were inexcusably careless. They were flying in unfamiliar territory, they were flying at night, and neither of them had any experience as a nighttime pilot. What's more, both of them knew they would have to come down sooner or later. Yet, in spite of the fact that they knew they were dangerously lost, they did not even bother to turn on the sophisticated instrument that was at their fingertips—the instrument that instantly would have shown them the direction to their destination.

As I finished the story, the young sailor burst out with, "I can't understand anyone being that foolish! Imagine having an omni that would have led them home and then not even using it!"

"You're right," I said, "they certainly were foolish. There was no excuse in the world for their dying. They knew they would have to land sometime and yet they didn't even turn to the omni to be sure they landed in the right place."

"But," I continued, "I wonder if they were any more foolish than you! You are on a flight through life. You have never gone this way before. You have never lived before. You know your life here on earth must end sometime. What's more, I have come to see you with a Bible in my hand. This Bible will tell you the course you ought to take. This Bible will show you the way to Heaven. Yet, you are not even interested in it. Even though this Heavenly Omni is right here at your fingertips, you are not even willing to turn it on!"

A few minutes later the three of us were bowed in prayer and the young man gave his heart to God. That night he and his wife attended the revival service and when the invitation was over he came forward to publicly acknowledge his faith in the Lord Jesus Christ.

The Bible Shows the Way

Good Neighbor, God has given us the Bible to guide us through life and lead us to Heaven. The Bible and only the Bible tells men how to be saved. Jesus Christ said,

"Jesus saith unto him, I am the way, the truth, and the life: no man cometh unto the Father, but by me."—John 14:6.

The way to Heaven, the Bible says, is the Lord Jesus Christ. The way to Heaven is not by joining a church or being baptized but is by trusting the Lord.

And the way to get the most out of life is to follow the teaching of the Bible. Proverbs 3:5,6 says,

"Trust in the LORD with all thine heart; and lean not unto thine own understanding. In all thy ways acknowledge him, and he shall direct thy paths."

We are to trust in the Lord—not trust in guesses, not trust in luck, not trust in our own wisdom. *"Lean not unto thine own understanding"* the Bible says.

Psalm 119:105 says, concerning the Bible,

"Thy word is a lamp unto my feet, and a light unto my path."

How foolish for any man to die without salvation when God has given us the Bible to show us the way to Heaven.

And how foolish for any Christian to live in sin, in misery, in unhappiness, in failure and defeat. We should trust in the Lord for our salvation and for our life as Christians. If we would but follow the teaching of the Bible, we would have happy marriages, successful businesses, godly children and a wonderful life!

A New Year

We are now facing a brand new year. We have never traveled this year before. We do not know what lies ahead—**but God does!** Let us commit our way to Him and be assured that this year He will direct our paths.

Texan's New Language

A YANKEE TEXAN WHO COULD OUT-CUSS, OUT-DRINK AND OUT-GAMBLE ANY MAN IN TOWN, MET THE SKY PILOT'S SAVIOUR AND HAD A PROBLEM WITH OLD BLACKIE.

It was during a revival in Indiana that everyone was asking if I had met Butch. He was from Texas, and it was generally known that he was the cussingest, drinkingest, meanest man in town. He and his wife, a young couple, lived an openly sinful life. They regularly had drinking parties for their friends that were so wicked I could not even tell a group of men about them. He probably bought more window glass than any man in town because he and his drunken guests often threw empty whiskey bottles out through the windows in his home without bothering to first raise the glass.

It was a hot summer morning that I walked down to see Butch. He was mowing his lawn. I could not help but be impressed with his ruggedly handsome looks, his fine shoulders, black wavy hair and white teeth. His disposition was not very pretty, though. He was grouchy and unfriendly.

"Hello, there," I grinned.

"H'lo," he said without stopping or looking up.

"I'd like to talk with you a little. My name's Bill Rice."

"You the Sky Pilot?" he asked, still without looking or stopping.

"Yes."

"Might talk about Texas," I said. "I was raised there and understand you were."

"Texas!" His entire attitude underwent an immediate change. "You from Texas? What part?"

He dropped the lawn mower and walked briskly over to shake hands. We were friends at once. In fact, we were almost bosom buddies for the Brotherhood of Texas is probably the world's largest fraternity. We ambled over to a shade tree and sat down under it. Then the Texas talk began.

We talked about horses—Quarter Horses mostly.

We talked about boots—Hyer boots, Nacona boots and Justin boots.

We talked about guns—Winchester, Savage and Marlin rifles and Colt and Smith & Wesson six-guns.

We talked hunted and fishing and weather and camp fires.

But one thing greatly marred my own enjoyment of the conversation. Butch was—I am serious—the cussingest one man I have ever heard cuss. He absolutely could not say anything at all without using filthy, obscene language. He used the Lord's name tied on to every nasty word I think I have ever heard. Usually, I speak at once about cussing to anyone I have a conversation with, but in this case, I did not speak to him at once but waited for an opportune time.

The time soon came.

Water From the Well

Before we knew it, it was noon and Butch's wife was hollering for him to come to dinner.

"Got enough for an extra?" he asked.

"Who?" his wife wanted to know.

"This feller," Butch told her.

"Who's he?"

"A feller from Texas."

"Bring him in!"

Sin had left no more of a mark in her face than in his. She was a tough sister, and she dead sure looked it. But she was friendly to me because I was a fellow Texan. I was shocked that her language was almost as filthy as his and prayed to God to give me wisdom and spiritual power to be a blessing to them.

Before we sat down to eat, she told him to go to the well for water. He picked up a large white pitcher, and I offered to go with him to the well. He held the pitcher under the water spout, and I pumped the cool, clear water until the pitcher was brimful. We turned to go back into the house when a large, shaggy, black dog came bounding around the corner of this house. It was Blackie, Butch's dog, that rushed joyfully to greet him.

Butch was stripped to the waist, and when Blackie got to his master he reared up, hitting the pitcher with his front paws and splashing the cold water over Butch's bare chest and stomach.

The water was so cold it took Butch's breath away—but he soon recovered. In an angry roar, he said, "Blackie you _____" and there followed such a string of filthy cussing as I have seldom heard in all my life. He was still yelling obscenities long after Blackie, tail tucked between his legs, had disappeared out of sight back around the corner of the house.

With his face still an angry red, Butch turned to me and half-apologetically said, "I'm sorry to cuss so much in front of you, but that dog just doesn't understand any other language!"

I told him he ought to apologize to God for it was a serious thing to take His name in vain *"...for the Lord will not hold him guiltless that taketh his name in vain."* And I reminded him that *"...everyone of us must give an account of himself unto God."*

We went back into the house for dinner.

Mrs. Butch's Conversion

At the table he said, "You see what we have—dive in."

"How about me praying first," I suggested. "I always have prayer before I eat, and if you don't care, I'll pray and thank God for this food."

Butch's reply was friendly, but his language was vile. "You can pray if you want," he said, "I don't give a blankety blank blank whether you do or not."

I prayed and while I thanked God for the food, I also thanked Him for Jesus, the Bread from Heaven, who can satisfy the soul of hunger of those who trust in Him. After the meal, we retired to the living room and I spoke plainly with them about their sins and need of the Saviour.

It seemed like I didn't get to first base with either, and when I asked them to at least come to church, she said she didn't think she would, and he said he knew blankety blank good and well he wouldn't.

But both of them were in the service that very night!

He came several times after that, and she came every night during the rest of the meeting. It was the last Sunday morning that she came forward at the invitation time with tears rolling down her face. "I love Butch, and if I quit drinking and going to wild parties, I just know he will leave me," she sobbed, "but I am not going to Hell for any man—not even for Butch." I carefully explained God's plan of salvation to her again and prayed with her. She was greatly comforted about herself but still miserable in her concern over her husband. We agreed to pray for him.

Much Obliged, Lord

She came back for the closing service, and he came with her. At the conclusion of the message, there was a good response to the invitation, but Butch did not come forward. Neither did he leave during the invitation as he had previously done. He hung around until everyone else had shaken my hand and left the building. Plainly, there was something on his mind, for when I walked back to talk with him, he stood with his hands in his pockets and looking at his feet and turning and twisting as though embarrassed.

"What's on your mind?" I asked.

He hesitated a bit and then finally blurted out, "Bill, is it too late?" (Actually, he said, "too blamed late.")

"Too late for what, Butch?" I asked, although I was sure I knew what he meant.

"Too late to get what my wife got!" he answered.

"You mean you want to be saved?"

"Yes."

"You mean you are willing to turn from your sins? Quit cussing and drinking and all the rest?"

"Yes," he answered. "I know I'm plenty mean, but I sure want to be saved if God will save me."

I took my Bible and explained how to be saved. He asked questions and we talked for a long time. Finally, I asked if he understood and still wanted to be saved, and he said he did.

"Let's get on our knees and ask God to save you," I suggested.

He hesitated, "Do I have to get on my knees?" he asked.

"You have been getting on your knees to shoot craps haven't you?" I asked.

"Yes."

"Then you dead sure aren't too good to get on your knees to ask God to forgive you!"

We got on our knees. (Now I know you don't have to get on your knees every time you pray, but in this case, I felt it would be good for him.)

I prayed and asked God to save him—then told him to pray. He said he didn't know how—he had never prayed in his life.

"Just ask God to save you," I suggested.

"Please save me, Lord," he prayed. That's all he said.

We got to our feet and I asked if he felt God had saved him, and he said he sure thought something had happened! I suggested we get back on our knees and thank the Lord, and he kneeled at once. I prayed first, thanking God for saving him. I asked him to pray.

"Much obliged, Lord," he said!

A New Language

That night after church, the Princess and I went to their home for a late supper. They had fixed some hot Texas chili, and while our wives warmed it up and set the table, Butch and I talked about the goodness of God. Finally, they called to tell us supper was on the table.

"Butch," his wife said, "we are out of water. Take the white pitcher out to the pump and fill it."

He took the pitcher, and he and I walked out to the pump behind the house and again he held the pitcher under the spout until it was brimful. And then again the big black dog came running around the corner of the house!

Again he went straight to his master and reared up on him in joyful welcome. Again, the water was splashed on Butch's chest and stomach only this time he was all dressed up in his Sunday-go-to meetin' suit! The water was so cold and Butch gasped as it drenched him, and to make matters worse, the pitcher was knocked from his hand and it broke to bits on the curbing of the well as it fell!

"Blackie!" he yelled when he could get his breath, "Blackie, you old—you—you—I'm—you—."

The dog, of course, had disappeared long before Butch finished stammering, trying to think of something suitable to say.

Finally, Butch, still waving his fist above his head, turned to look at me. In the light from the open kitchen door, I saw a sheepish, self-conscious grin spread over his face and then he said,

"I'll declare, Rice, I've got to teach that dog a new language, haven't I!"

A New Creation

And so it has been with many, many a man and woman. When the Lord Jesus comes in, many a person has had to learn new words and habits. The Bible says,

"Therefore if any man be in Christ, he is a new creature: old things are passed away; behold, all things are become new."—II Corinthians 5:17.

The word "creature," in the Greek, actually means "creation." And when a sinner turns to Christ, God actually makes him a brand new creation. Old things do pass away and the wickedness he one time loved, he now hates, and the things of God he once hated, he now loves. Many a man who once was a drunkard is now a sober man because of the change Christ has wrought. Many a thief is now honest, many a liar now truthful, many unclean now virtuous since Jesus came into his heart.

For God works a miracle in the heart of one who trusts His son.

HUNGRY-HEARTED DEAF

I have just closed a wonderful revival campaign with the West End Presbyterian Church in Hopewell, Virginia. I do not know when I have been with a more wonderful group of people. The young pastor, a Wheaton grad, is a vigorous, enthusiastic, hard-working, soul-winning, Bible-believing Presbyterian.

All of my life I have heard the expression "like pastor like people." Through the years, I have found this to be generally true. It was certainly true in this case. Various committees really worked at the job and were eager to do everything they knew to help the revival. The volunteer choir came night after night without being begged to do so. The pianist and organist were not only present every night but came early enough for rehearsals.

The auditorium has a balcony that runs all the way down each side and across the back. The organ and the choir—believe it or not—are up on the rear balcony! I feel sure the fellow who dreamed that one up not only hated music but was a sheep herder to boot!

In spite of some bad weather, attendance was good night after night. And I do not remember a night when the invitation was given that there were not those who came forward. Sometimes two or three, sometimes ten or fifteen, sometimes more.

United Nations!

Fort Lee, Virginia is nearby. Officers come here from friendly nations all over the world the be trained in American battle technique.

One Friday night we had Army officers from the Philippines, Vietnam, Indonesia, Burma, Thailand and Liberia. They came in uniform and with all the medals and ribbons on their tunics made quite an imposing sight. The pastor said it looked like at least half the United Nations were present!

Although these officers came on time, the building was already packed and the ushers put extra chairs for them just inside the railing on the rear balcony. When the invitation was given, I noticed one of the officers bow to his companions, turn and walk through the door at the rear of the balcony. I supposed he was leaving the building, but a moment later he came through the downstairs door and walked down the aisle toward the front. The pastor was greeting others who were coming forward and I stepped from the platform to meet this gentleman. It turned out he was a major from Liberia and the only Negro to attend the meetings. I asked him why he had come forward and he said he had come to ask God to forgive him of his sins and to accept Jesus Christ as his Saviour.

After the closing service on Sunday night, a captain from Burma sought me out to say that he, too, had accepted Christ that night as his Saviour. He had not made up his mind until the invitation had closed, but he wanted me to know before I left.

High Spot of Campaign

But the high spot of the campaign for me was the night five adult deaf came. They had been told that I could speak Sign Language and that I was going to show pictures of the deaf who came to the Ranch last summer.

The first to come was an attractive young woman about twenty-one years of age. She came about forty-five minutes early. She worked in a bank in Richmond, Virginia. When I asked if she were married, she laughed and said no, she was an old maid. I told her she looked like a very young maid to me and assured her she would enjoy the pictures.

Next came a young man and his wife. He worked as a painter in a factory. A few minutes later another couple came.

We all sat down in the auditorium and visited for the next thirty minutes. I asked each of them if they were saved and each looked a bit puzzled but said that he was.

During the song service, I sat on the platform and gave them the words to Renstrom's solos and explained that I would have to stop talking with them when the time came for me to preach. One good thing about Sign Language—I could sit on the platform and still talk to them as they sat in the pews. And without drawing too much attention to the fact that we were having a conversation.

After the service, one of the fine young couples of the church invited the deaf to their home for refreshments. I told them I would come in thirty or forty minutes after I had finished at the church.

It was almost an hour before I was able to go to the home. I was surprised to see that not only these deaf but a good many others had dropped in and all were happily eating cake and ice cream! Where in the world that young couple got enough to feed such a group late at night I have no idea.

Anyway, we all stayed until twelve o'clock that night. Of course, I asked each of the deaf where they went to church, who their pastor was, when they had accepted Christ, etc. Whether any or all of them were saved, I do not know. If they had been saved they knew very little about Bible teaching.

But this I do know, they were not only the friendliest and nicest group you ever saw, but they seemed genuinely hungry for the Gospel. Each of them said they were going to try to get their vacation so they could come to the Ranch this summer and I do hope they will be able to come.

Soul Winners Needed

As I have often said before, the deaf right here in our own country comprise probably the greatest missionary opportunity in the whole world today. In the first place, **they are here**! About fifteen million of them. A missionary does not have to have a special educational requirements, special physical requirements, does not even have to leave this country in order to be a missionary among the deaf.

Of course, one should learn the Sign Language in order to work among the deaf. But it is probably far easier to speak Sign Language to the deaf than it would be to learn, for example, to speak in Chinese, Russian, Spanish or a South American or African dialect.

Easy to Win

The deaf are hungry for the Gospel of Jesus Christ. I am an evangelist and I deal with a good many thousands of people every year. I preach from the pulpit and I talk to individuals in homes, schools, jails and on the street. There is no question in the world about it. Deaf people are easier to win to Christ than any other group or individuals in America.

Feed the Hungry

When men do not have bread, they hunger for it. When they do not have water, they thirst for it. Jesus said,

"And Jesus said unto them, I am the bread of life: he that cometh to me shall never hunger; and he that believeth on me shall never thirst."—John 6:35.

If a hungry man came to your door you certainly would not turn him away without feeding him. If a man were dying of thirst, you would surely give him a drink. And yet, Good Neighbor, people are dying around us every day—dying without bread, without water. They are the deaf who do not know the Lord Jesus Christ.

Surely it would please the Lord if all of us had a part in Cumberwood's (Bill Rice Ranch) ministry to the deaf. Prospects for the future have never looked brighter. Sunday school classes for the deaf are being organized in churches across the land. Many fine young Christians indicate they will come this summer to begin learning Sign Language in order that they may work with the deaf.

WHERE'S THE TAIL AT?

De-ticking the Cattle

A vicious blood-sucking insect infests the trees of West Texas. During the hot summer months these ticks get on the cattle and not only make them lose flesh but often transmit a disease called tick fever. So, in order to get rid of these ticks, ranchers dip their cattle each year in a water solution.

The dipping vat is usually made of poured concrete and is about two and a half feet wide and fifteen feet long. At the near end it is five feet deep while at the far end the bottom slopes up to make a ramp. This vat is filled with water and then chemicals are added that will kill ticks or wood lice or fleas or any other insect that happens to be on the cattle.

The steers walk down a chute to the near end of the vat. They are forced to jump into the water and they dive in over their heads. They immediately come up and swim to the far side. As soon as their feet touch the ramp, they simply walk on up and into the pen on the far side.

One season Dad and the ranch hands were dipping a herd of cattle. My brothers John and George, of course, were helping. It had been a long day and everyone was tired. Make no mistake about it, working with stock is just plain hard work. Cattle must be rounded up and herded into corrals. Then they must be driven single file, down the long chute that leads to the dipping vat. When a steer gets to the edge of the vat, he inevitably applies his brakes and then throws himself into reverse! A pole is quickly thrust horizontally across the chute to act as a gate and bar his full retreat. The chute makes a lane that is too narrow for a steer to turn around in. He is then persuaded to plunge into the water.

Sometimes the men on foot simply cannot force a steer to jump into the vat. It then becomes necessary for a cowboy to ride a horse into the pen at the far end of the vat, rope the balky steer and then literally drag him into the water.

On this particular afternoon, everyone was just about tuckered out. It had been a long, hot, hard day and the men would be glad when the last steer had been dunked in the tick-killing vat. It was then that an ornery old cow with a stubborn nature and fighting disposition was herded into the chute. With her first footstep, she showed that she intended to cause just as much trouble as possible. The men had to pull and shove her every step of the way down the long chute. When they finally got her to the water's edge, she simply threw a double-barreled tantrum.

George happened to be working at the edge of the vat at the time and no matter what he tried, he simply could not get that old cow into the water! The more he pushed and pried, the more she resisted and the madder he got. Of course, someone could have mounted a horse, gone to the other pen, roped her around the horns and dragged her in. But this would take time and George was determined that he was going to get her into that water or know the reason why.

In her struggle to retreat, the old cow backed into the bar-pole with such force that it broke. She continued to go in reverse and George shoved another bar-pole behind her. But he put it too low and she tripped over it, sat down in the chute, and then flopped over on her back. Meanwhile, cowboys back down at the opening of the chute were forcing other steers in and the result was that a big steer who had been following the cow promptly walked on over her and then stopped at the edge of the vat. The old cow finally struggled to her feet but now she was heading in the wrong direction.

George was fit to be tied! The steer now first in line was a big fellow, much larger than the cow that was now backed tail to tail against him. George had an angry inspiration. He was determined to show that cow what was what and who was who! He was going to get her in the water whether she went in head first or tail first.

So he quickly reached between the rails of the fence and tied the two tails together.

He would make the big steer drag that cow hind end first into the dipping vat!

With a loud yell he punched the big steer in the rump with a stick and the steer gave a mighty leap into the water. Under he went—head, horns, hoof and all—then came to the top and swam to the far end, but the old cow had not gone backwards into the water. When the steer gave his great leap, there had been a loud snap but the old cow had not moved a foot nearer the edge of the vat.

George stared in unbelief. What in the world had happened? If their tails had been tied together and one had gone into the water, why hadn't the other been dragged in too? And then he suddenly knew the answer to his question. His eyes bugged out as he pointed to the old cow's rump and yelled, "Where'd her tail go! Where's her tail at!"

"Thar it goes," yelled one of the cowboys pointing to the big steer who was now walking out of the big vat at the far end. Like Little Bo Peep's sheep, he was wagging his tail behind him. In fact, he was wagging two tails behind him—his own and the one tied to it that had belonged to the ornery old cow.

It had pulled her tail off!

Later, when Dad and George marched out to the barn, George was grateful for at least one thing—this time when Dad informed him he was going to get his pants spanked, he knew better than to take them off first!

Angry Decisions Are Often Wrong Ones

I heard Dr. John tell this story in a sermon when I was just nine years old. I asked Dad about it and he told me that George had certainly known better than to tie those two bovines' tails together, but he had been so mad he could not think straight. My dad went on to say that it was usually a bad mistake to make decisions based on anger, and Dad went on to talk to me about my hot temper. He reminded me that I often said things, in anger, that I did not really mean. He reminded me that I sometimes let my temper get me into fights with my best friends. He said that if I didn't learn to control my temper, it would cause me trouble all of my life.

And you know what—my Dad was a prophet! It was not until after I had surrendered to preach that I really began trying to control my temper. I suppose my temper has caused me more trouble than any other part of my personality. And I suppose I have prayed more about being able to control my temper than about resisting any other sin in my life.

A man under the influence of anger may sin as horribly and make as big a fool of himself as a man under the influence of liquor!

ROOMMATES

THE TRUE STORY OF A COUPLE OF YOUNG TEXANS WHO HAD BEEN "BEST FRIENDS" AS BOYS AND PLANNED TO GO THROUGH COLLEGE TOGETHER.

In a little Texas town, there lived two boys—let us call them Tom and Bill. In high school, they were the warmest of friends. Tom was a star athlete and excelled in football, basketball, running and so on. He was not especially handsome but always dressed neatly and expensively and was the most popular boy in the ninth grade. His parents were fairly well-to-do.

Bill was not popular, was not a good athlete and his parents could not afford even nice clothing for him. But he and Tom loved one another sincerely and were inseparable friends.

Then came the day that Bill's parents died, and Bill had to leave the little town to go to West Texas where he was to finish school. It was a sad day when he and Tom told one another good-bye, but they both agreed that they would finish high school and then both attend Decatur College where they would be roommates. And this they did.

When the time came that both had been graduated from high school, they both went to Decatur Baptist College and were roommates. They could not pal around together as much as formerly, however, because Bill had to work for his room and board and tuition. He milked cows, laundered shirts for other college boys, worked in a grocery store and did odd jobs. Tom's parents paid his way and he did not work but spent a few hours studying and a good many hours having one whale of a good time. As in high school, he became a great favorite with his classmates, and when the college annual came out, he had a prominent place as a student most likely to succeed in life.

And then came the night that Tom staggered to their room drunk. He was thoroughly ashamed of himself as Bill helped him into bed and, through drunken tears, vowed that he would never touch another drop of liquor. But he did. He ran around with the same gang, and it was not long until he not only drank habitually but said he saw no harm in it and urged Bill to drink, too.

It was not long afterwards that Tom came home one night after a date with his gang and confessed to Bill that he had, that night, gone into deeper sin. He blushed and told his roommate that he had gone into adultery. He was ashamed of himself and said he would never, never do it again. But he did and before long, he was declaring he saw nothing wrong in a "little fun" and was urging Bill to join up with his gang and have "fun," too.

He had also picked up the gambling habit.

Tom told Bill that his gang was teasing him because he had a "parson" for a roommate. He told Bill to either join up with him and his gang, or he would find another roommate.

They were tough days for Bill. His parents had been Christians and had led him to Christ when he was but a boy. They had taught him the Bible and warned him that his sins would find him out. And yet he envied Tom with all his heart. Tom didn't wear overalls to college classrooms—he bought swell clothes with gambling money. And Tom was so happy-go-lucky—he never worried about money he owed; he let the other fellow worry about it! And Tom was having a glorious time running around with his loose-moraled gang. Furthermore, Tom was sinning and getting by with it! He was still the most popular boy on the campus.

It was a hard battle for Bill, but finally he made his decision: he would stay by the teaching of God and the Bible like Mother and Father had taught him. He told Tom of his decision, and Tom moved to another room and another roommate. Bill faced the heartless teasing of other students who called him "Deacon" or "Reverend" or "Father." Most of them had never cared too much for Bill anyway, this young fellow who so often came to class in overalls and who did not even own a complete suit of clothes.

At the end of the year, both boys left college and did not make any effort to keep track of one another. Bill entered the ministry, spent two years in preparation, married a lovely girl and became pastor of a little church. After a time, a baby was born into his home, and Bill was supremely happy. He was in the Lord's work, was pastor of a growing church, had a wonderful wife and precious baby—what more could any man want?

When their baby was three months old, Bill took his little family to a Bible conference in Ft. Worth. He drove up to the church, his wife and baby went inside and he was locking the car when he noticed a bum leaning against a light post across the street. As he turned to go into the building, someone yelled, "Bill!" He turned and looked but saw no one he knew among the throng passing by. The bum was now walking across the street towards him. He turned again to enter the building when again someone yelled, "Hey, Bill!" Again he turned, and again he saw no one he knew. He was turning away again when the bum stepped up on the sidewalk and cried, "Bill—Bill! Don't you know me, Bill?" He swept his battered hat from his head and sandy hair fell down across his forehead, and Bill recognized him—it was Tom! Tom, who had been the most popular boy on the college campus! Tom, who thought he could sin and get by with it! Tom who was now a bum on the streets of Ft. Worth! Tom, whose sin had found him out!

Bill put his arm around his old friend as the school-day love, mingled with pity, flooded his heart. They went to the Y.M.C.A. where Bill bought Tom food, a bath, a shave and haircut and had his clothes cleaned up. He talked to him of God who loved sinners so much He gave His only Son to die for them and Tom accepted the Lord Jesus Christ as his Saviour, trusting Jesus to forgive his sins and save his soul.

THE HORSE I WOULDN'T RIDE

HE WAS A WILD-EYED, BUSHY-TAILED SON OF A BROOM-TAILED FILLY BUT I FELT SURE I COULD RIDE HIM...I DIDN'T!

Not long ago, while flying in an airplane, I read an article by a man who claimed he could remember being in his mother's womb before he was born!

That's right. This man claimed he could distinctly remember how it felt to be an unborn baby. He remembered, he said, the blackness, the warmth, the wetness and how it felt to be jostled around.

Personally, I just don't believe the fellow. But whether or not he could remember that far back, I dead sure can't. I can remember some things that happened when I was a very small boy, but I am not sure if the things I remember happened when I was two years old or if they happened when I was three years old.

I do not remember learning to talk.

I do not remember learning to walk.

I do not remember learning to ride a horse.

But one of the very first things I can remember was riding a horse with my father. He held me in front of him on the saddle and we rode up to the back of the ranch house. My mother came out the kitchen door and through the back yard gate and lifted me down from the saddle.

I do not remember the first time I rode a horse all by myself but I suppose it was when I was three years old.

I was four years old when we moved to Decatur, Texas and I remember riding Grandfather's black carriage horse, Buttons, in the pasture back of Grandfather's huge house.

Ability With Horses

I have often said—and more seriously than most realize—that I can do only three things effectively: work hard, tell an interesting story and handle a horse!

By the time I was eleven years old, I was breaking Shetland ponies. By the time I was thirteen years old, I was breaking and training cow horses.

Although our house was just four blocks from the city square, we had a ten-acre pasture back of our house. It was a rare thing I did not have one or two horses in this pasture that I was training. There were occasions when I had as many as seven. A rancher or farmer would bring me a horse to break and train. He would either pay me ten dollars and furnish feed for the horse while I kept him or he would furnish feed and let me keep the horse for one year. In this way, I always had a good riding horse without it costing Dad anything.

Until I was a senior in high school, I was always small for my age. Many people, especially those who knew nothing about horses, marveled that a small, skinny, cotton-headed little boy could handle a thousand-pound horse. But I had learned that one does not handle a horse with sheer strength. You handle a horse by leverage. You handle him with a rope while you are on the ground and with the reins and bit when you are on his back!

The Graham Ranch

Mother and Father both died when I was in my teens and a half sister, Mrs. Ruth Martin, invited me to come and live with her and her three little boys. She taught school on the Graham ranch between Olney and Archer City, Texas. It would be good for the boys, she said, to have a "man" around the house.

I drove her new Ford car to Olney each day and after school and on Saturdays, I often rode with some of the hands on the ranch; and during this time, my sister was being courted by a neighboring rancher named Millard Martin. They were married shortly after I was graduated from high school.

Back to Texas!

In the years that followed, I spent a year at Decatur Baptist College, went to Dallas where I worked for my splendid big brother, Dr. John R. Rice, was pastor in Gainesville, Texas and during that pastorate, the Princess and I were married. Then we went to Moody Bible Institute in Chicago.

When Christmas came, we found it was possible to go to Texas over the holidays. After visiting with Cathy's folks and the John Rices and Joe Rices and the Nuttings (another wonderful half sister), we drove to Archer County to visit the Martin ranch. After visiting a while, Mr. Martin said to me, "Let's go out to the corral. I have something I want to show you."

In the corral there was a powerful bay horse about three years old. We stepped into the corral and Mr. Martin handed me a rope. I threw it over the horse's neck and—he exploded! Obviously this horse had never been handled very much and certainly had never been ridden.

"Think you can ride him?" Mr. Martin asked.

"He might give me a little trouble at first," I replied, "but I think I could stay on him all right."

"I sure would appreciate it if you would top him for me," Mr. Martin said. "There's no one around here to do it."

"Be glad to," I said. "Where's your saddle?"

We put the saddle on a fence between us and began unlacing the stirrup leathers. I am a tall, long-legged man and Mr. Martin was a short man. We would have to lengthen the stirrups as long as we could to make them fit me.

While we were unlacing the strings, the Princess, leading Betty who was just beginning to walk, came out to the corral.

"What are you doing?" she asked.

"We are lengthening these stirrups," I told her, "so I can ride that horse for Mr. Martin."

Just then, the horse that was snubbed to a hitching post began screaming and kicking and fighting the rope.

My lovely young wife was plainly startled and Betty was so scared she began to cry.

"Is that horse tame?" the Princess asked.

"No," I replied. "He has never been ridden. But he is going to be a great deal tamer in just a few minutes!"

"You mean you are going to get on that horse?"

"Of course I am," I said. "Mr. Martin needs someone to top that horse for him and this is the first chance I have had for a long time to ride a bucking bronc."

The Princess stood silent for a moment, just watching us unlace those rawhide strings. Then she quietly said, "Sweetheart, you are not a boy any longer. You are a grown man with a wife and baby and a ministry and school to consider. I know you think you can ride that horse, but if you should get hurt it could mean you would have to drop out of school for this semester and it would take at least six months later to graduate. It would be at least six months later before you could become a full-time evangelist. And if you were hurt—what would Betty and I do?

"I don't know much about horses and this one scares me. But I don't believe you can afford to ride that horse just for the fun of it."

With that she and Betty turned and walked hand in hand back toward the ranch house. I was silent for a minute and then turned to Mr. Martin.

"She's right," I said. I walked into the corral and released the struggling horse. Then Mr. Martin and I readjusted the stirrups to fit him and put the saddle away.

It Was Not Worth What It Would Have Cost

Actually, I did not doubt then and I do not doubt now but that I could have ridden that horse. Of course, I would have felt the effects of it for a couple of days. It is one thing to ride a bucking horse for ten seconds in a rodeo, and it is another thing to ride a bucking horse until he either throws you or he simply cannot buck any longer. The terrific jolting does strange things to a feller's innards and he is likely to be pretty sore for a while. But that's the least of the possible consequences of riding a bucking horse. There is always the danger of getting thrown on your head or getting a broken arm or leg or back. And if the bronc cannot throw you, he may decide to slam you into the fence or rear up and fall over backwards on top of you.

I know what it is to ride a bucking horse and be sick for several hours afterwards and sore for a couple of days afterwards. And I know what it is to be skinned up by being rubbed against the fence, to be thrown hard and once to have an arm knocked out of place.

I would have enjoyed riding that horse, but the Princess was right—it might have cost far, far more than the fun was worth.

Be Sure It's the Right Fun at the Right Price

This is a profitable lesson for any young man or woman to learn. Last week two teenage boys were killed in a car wreck not far from the Bill Rice Ranch. They were driving 80 miles an hour in a 45-mile zone—just for fun! But the "fun" wasn't worth it—it cost the boys their lives.

A teenage boy was caught shoplifting. He told the judge he had been stealing "just for fun." The boy was reprimanded and released. A few days afterward, he was again caught shoplifting. This time his girl friend was with him. And this time the boy received a sentence in the reformatory. He had been stealing "just for fun" but it turned out to be expensive fun. It may prevent him from being accepted in the right college or getting the right job later on in life.

I once knew a college boy who said that he was willing to "try anything once as long as it was fun." So he tried getting drunk. And he tried it again—and again—and again. The last time I saw him, several years later, he was a drunkard who has lost his wife and job and self respect and will power. He paid entirely too much for his fun.

Again and again we read of high school kids going to "pot parties" where they experiment with dope that may well ruin their lives. They simply do not consider the cost before they decide dope is fun.

And, for that matter, the boy or girl who begins smoking cigarettes just for fun does not dream what it may cost him or her in the long run.

To Be Mature Is to Be Responsible

When all is said and done, the one thing that separates the men from the boys is the willingness to accept responsibility. To face up to obligations. To put the will of God ahead of personal desire. Romans 14:12 says,

"So then every one of us shall give account of himself to God."

It is foolish to do something that may bring pleasure for a moment but may also cost a broken body or a ruined life that will bring sorrow for years and years to come. Now, everyone who knows me knows that I am not an overly cautious man. I believe in taking chances when it is not simply a matter of recklessness or selfishness but to honor Christ. But it is foolish to risk one's future for the sake of some thrill, some pleasure that—even if it is not necessarily wicked—is likely to cost far more than it is ever worth. Jesus said,

"And he said to them all, If any man will come after me, let him deny himself, and take up his cross daily, and follow me." (Luke 9:23)

A NIGHT ON A TEXAS RANCH THAT CHANGED MY LIFE

I LEFT THE RANCH ON A BEAUTIFUL SILVER HORSE, A BORROWED SADDLE, NOT ONE CENT IN MY POCKET—AND SCARED HALF TO DEATH! I WAS GOING TO COLLEGE....

Early one morning before daylight, I slapped a saddle on the back of the large silver horse, Go West. Both the horse and I were sore and stiff. I was sore because the day before I had tried to ride the Silver Outlaw and she had thrown me sky high.

And I do mean she had **thrown** me! Any astronaut would have been jealous. In less than one minute, I had experienced blast-off, gone into orbit, made a re-entry and crash landed! And that was why I was sore and stiff.

But after she had thrown me, Go West met a man she couldn't throw. He was a young Texan named Wes Harden. Wes was a champion bronc buster and he was a man the big horse couldn't throw. She bucked all over that corral. Men had tried to ride her when she was two years old but several had been hurt, one seriously. After that she had been turned loose on the ranch and had roamed free for the last five years. So, she was not accustomed to the strenuous work of bucking. Moreover, after Wes had taken the fight out of her, he had let her run across the prairie at breakneck speed until she was exhausted. So, Go West was as stiff and as sore as I was.

That's why I wasn't afraid of her bucking with me that morning, and she was gong to be too tired to do any bucking on the long ride from the Graham Ranch to Decatur, Texas.

Going to College!

The story I am going to tell you is one of the best stories I know. It is a true story about an event that changed my life, and it has changed the lives of thousands of people who have heard me tell it, for I have told this story in many revival campaigns, radio broadcasts, printed it in the **Sword of the Lord** and in the booklet,

"The Land of Beginning Again."

I was born in a little three-room ranch house near Dundee, Texas. The old house is not there any more since it burned down years ago.

We moved to Decatur, Texas when I was just a little boy four years old. When I was in my teens, both my mother and my father died.

They left me more than enough money to get a college education. Since I was a teenager, the state appointed a guardian who was a mighty good man. If I had been given my choice of someone to be my guardian, he is probably the man I would have selected.

My widowed sister, Ruth, invited me to live with her on the big Graham Ranch. My sister, a wonderful woman, taught school. She and her three little boys—her husband had died several years earlier—and I lived in one room of the schoolhouse and she taught school in the other, and I drove her Ford car every day to Olney, Texas and graduated from high school there.

After finishing high school, I wanted to go to college, but my guardian had loaned my inheritance to men who never repaid it and there were no funds left for a college education. The more I thought about it, the more I felt I ought to go to college and should at least try. It was in the depression and jobs were hard to find, but I was willing to work hard and I felt sure I could get money for board and room and tuition some way or other.

Every bit of clothing—everything I had in the world—I put into an old suitcase that had belonged to my father. It took exactly every penny I had to mail that thing to Decatur, Texas! I did not have a penny—not a red cent left, but I was going to college or know the reason why!

Three Meals in One and a Bed

So in the blackness of early morning, I saddled the beautiful silver horse, Go West, with a saddle I had borrowed from Arlie Bearden, stepped into the saddle and left the Graham Ranch. I can still remember waving good-bye, in the blackness of that early dawn, to the schoolhouse up on the hill, the ranch house where the

Grahams lived, the barn and stable and other buildings. When I reached the highway, I turned left toward Archer City and Decatur a hundred miles or more away.

Most of the time I rode just off the shoulder of the highway. There were other times, however, when I could take short cuts across unfenced prairies.

I rode on until noon. Go West was an easy-riding horse with a smooth, steady fox trot. By noon I had gone about 25 miles beyond Archer City.

When the sun was high overhead, I stopped at a pond beside the highway. I unsaddled Go West, let her drink and then let her graze for an hour. The sun was hot and I realized how tired and sore I was as I watched the silver one.

After an hour, I again slapped the saddle on Go West and stepped into the saddle. I was hot and tired and hungry and just plain scared. I had told everyone that I was going to college, but talk is cheap. I did not have any money, and where was I going to stay tonight?

All through that long, hot Texas afternoon, I became more uneasy and began getting bitter and backslidden.

My dad had read the Bible again and again at night, around the fireplace, when he and Mother were alive. He had told me again and again, "Now, Son, you live for God. You will be glad you did." And yet I was living for the Lord. I had never danced, never smoked, never tasted any kind of liquor, never committed adultery, never stolen. And yet, what did it get me? A "good" Christian had borrowed my money and would not pay it back and here I was without a meal, a home or a penny!

And as the long hot afternoon wore on, I became more bitter and backslidden in my heart. I said to myself, "This Sunday school business is not for me. When I get to Decatur, I am going to live like everyone else."

The afternoon was long and hot and dusty. Then, along towards evening, the sky became clouded over, lightning flashed and thunder rolled.

What a time to be on the open prairie! I was going to get sopping wet along with my horse and saddle, and it would probably rain all night!

Presently, I hit the old highway from Jacksboro to Decatur. On the left of the highway there was a great big place with a large white house and big barns. I turned off the highway up a little gravel lane to the gate of a white picket fence. It began sprinkling rain as I yelled, "Hello."

A gray-haired man came to the door of the house. He called, "Hello, yourself. Get down." I got off the horse and walked up the path and he walked to meet me in the sprinkle of rain.

"I am going to Decatur," I told him. "I am going to go to college there." I was so proud of the fact that I was going to college. "It is going to rain," I continued, "and I wonder if you would care if I just stayed in your barn tonight?"

He said, "Well, I would not care at all, young fellow, but I do have a whole year's crop in that barn. Don't strike any matches. You don't smoke, do you?"

"No sir," I said. "I don't smoke and I will not strike any matches."

"What did you say your name was?" he asked.

I had not told him but now I did. I said, "My name is Bill Rice and I am going to Decatur to go to college."

"Rice?" he asked.

"Yes."

He said, "Are you any kin to the old Senator Rice that used to live in Decatur?"

"Yes sir," I said. "He was my father."

"Your father!"

"Yes sir."

He turned around and yelled, "Hey, Ma! Ma!"

A gray-haired lady came to the door and he yelled, "Ma, you will never guess who this young fellow is. He is Wil Rice's son. He is going to stay all night with us. Get the vittles back on the table."

She smiled and called to me, "We are so glad to see you, Son. You come on in and I will feed you."

First we went to the barn and unsaddled Go West and gave her oats, hay and fresh water. We ran to the house through a downpour of rain to find she had put supper back on the table. Actually, I have forgotten just what it was but I imagine that it was corn bread, turnip greens and black-eyed peas and good things like that.

While I was at it, I ate breakfast, dinner and supper!

While I was finishing the meal, they put a bed—springs and mattress and fresh sheets—down on the front porch.

The good lady said, "Now, Bill, you are going to have a long ride tomorrow. You better get to bed."

We walked out onto the porch—the rain had stopped—and the old rancher said, "Ma, let's get ready for bed out on the front porch."

Well, that sounded odd to me. Getting ready for bed, as far as I was concerned, meant undressing and putting on your night clothes. But that wasn't what the man had meant. This gray-haired rancher fell on his knees and the gray-haired lady knelt beside him there on the front porch. In the moonlight he lifted his head toward the sky and prayed, "O God, we don't want to go to sleep tonight until we have talked to you again."

I fell to my backslidden knees. This man prayed for his two sons and two daughters—I have two sons and two daughters today—and he prayed for his friends, for his grandchildren, then he prayed for me and asked that I might have a good night's rest and be glad I had stopped to spend the night with them.

I pulled off my boots and got undressed and crawled into bed. I still remember the clean sheets and how good they felt and smelled.

The bed was soft, the air was fresh and sweet smelling and I was dog-tired. I immediately went to sleep.

Loving Kindness and Tender Mercies

It seemed I had hardly fallen asleep when the old gentleman was shaking me by the shoulder as he said, "You'd better get up, Bill. It will be daylight soon and you have a long ride ahead of you. Come around to the pump at the kitchen door and we will wash up."

It was pitch dark as I sat up and began feeling around for my boots and clothes. As soon as I finished dressing, I walked around to the kitchen door and he was waiting by the pump. I pumped water and he washed, and he pumped and I washed. The water was like ice!

Then we went in for breakfast and—man alive! There was fried chicken, biscuits and cowboy gravy!

I ate longer than they did. When they finished eating, she began making a lunch for me to take with me that day. In the meantime, he went out to the barn and fed Go West, saddled her and brought her up to the front yard gate.

I had just finished eating the last piece of chicken and sopping up the gravy on my plate when he came back into the house. He was wearing overalls. He reached into the bib pocket and pulled out a pencil and a checkbook.

"Bill," he said, "you are going to need some money if you are going to college. How much money do you think you will need this first year?"

Neighbor, I simply could not believe my ears! I had just met these folks last night. I did not know them and they did not know me, and here he was with a checkbook asking how much money it was going to take for my first year in college! I simply could not believe it.

I just sat there dumbfounded. When I could finally speak, I said,

"Well, I-ah-ah—you don't owe me any money. I don't want you giving me money."

"But," he said, "I would like to help you."

"Thank you," I said, "but I just do not want you giving me money."

"Well," he said, "if you doesn't want to take it as a gift, take it as a loan. Now, how much money do you want to borrow to pay for this first year of college?"

I still could not believe my ears! And, Good Neighbor, I'll tell you something you won't believe—I didn't let him give or loan me a cent! I said, "My dad taught me that if I borrow money, I have to pay it back, and I don't know when I would ever be able to pay you back. So, I am not going to borrow any money, either."

"But, Son, we can afford to lend you the money."

"Thank you," I said, "but I don't think I ought to borrow any money from you. I don't know when I could ever pay it back."

I did not—on my word of honor—take one cent.

But if the old rancher did not give me money, he gave me something I needed more. He gave me confidence. Not confidence in myself but in God. He made me realize the dear Lord had not forgotten me! He was standing by! My Heavenly Father knew I would not take the money and I know He knew it! But I knew something else, too—I knew my Heavenly Father was watching over me!

The Lord knew about those men who had talked my guardian out of my inheritance. The dear Lord knew I needed to find a job even though any kind of work was hard to find. But I needed a place to sleep and I needed food to eat and I needed money for books and tuition and I felt sure that my Heavenly Father was going to take care of me in these needs.

"Surely," I felt I could say with David, *"goodness and mercy shall follow me all the days of my life..."* (Psalm 23:6).

The "Tall Stranger" Who Had Been There Before Me

The old couple walked down the path toward the gate with me. It was just barely beginning to get light. Go West, the silver mare, was tied by the gate waiting for me to step into the saddle.

I stopped and thanked the couple with silver hair and generous hearts. She said to me, "You're welcome," and he said. "Don't even mention it."

I looked at them for a moment and then said, "Why have you been so good to me? Surely you don't take everybody into your home and feed them and give them a good bed and then try to give them money."

The rancher smiled and said, "Bill, I was going to tell you about this before I let you leave this morning."

"Some years ago, Ma and I came with our babies and made a down payment on this place. Then a depression came because of a long drought. We could not meet our payments. Water holes for the stock dried up and we couldn't raise a crop. A year passed and then another year passed. All of this time we could not pay a dime on our mortgage. We just barely could get a living.

"Finally, the fellow at the bank said, 'Look, we do not want to mistreat you, but we have to have some money. Our board of directors says we must collect something from you or we are simply going to be forced to foreclose.'

"Ma and I did not know what in the world we would do. We simply had no money to pay the bank. We wondered what would happen to us and to our babies. The men at the bank had been kind to us but finally a day was set that we must have money or the bank would be forced to foreclose on the ranch. I tried and tried to find work but there was not work to be found. We just did not know what was going to become of us.

"Then, one day, a Tall Stranger came riding a horse down this same highway. He rode up the lane just like you did, and that Tall Fellow told us he had heard we were in trouble and that he wanted to help us. He went with me down to the bank in Jacksboro and they knew him. He said to the banker,

"'This man has a wife and babies. He is an honest man but he just can't find work. Please don't take his ranch but let me go on his note. I will stand security for him because I know he will pay you as soon as he can. Please don't take his ranch.'

"That Tall Fellow signed the note and we got to keep the ranch. Later on we got it paid for.

"But that wasn't all the Tall Stranger did for us. He rode back out here and told my wife the good news about getting to keep the ranch. Then that Tall Fellow said he wanted to talk to me and my wife and the children for a few minutes. So my wife and I and the four children met in that parlor. That Tall Fellow took a Bible out of his pocket and he said to me, 'Now look, you are in danger of losing a lot more than a ranch. You are going to lose your soul if you do not find someone to help you save it.'

"And he told us about Jesus Christ!

"After he told us how to get saved, Ma and me and the kids who were old enough got down on our knees—right there in that parlor—and trusted Christ to save us. We were all saved and the Tall Stranger got on his horse and rode away.

"Bill, we have lived for the Lord ever since. My children grew up and got married and I gave every one of them a farm for a wedding present. God has been so good to us, but I would have lost the ranch and I would probably have lost my soul if it had not been for a man who heard we were in trouble and he came out here and just helped us.

"Bill, that Tall Stranger was your father!"

It Pays to Serve Jesus

My father! God bless him! Some forty years before, long before I was born, he had heard of a man in trouble and because my dad loved the Lord, he helped a man who was in need. Dad helped him save his ranch and then led him to Jesus Christ.

But my dad did not dream that some forty years later his baby boy—bitter, backslidden, broke, hungry and scared half to death— my daddy did not dream that I would ride down that very same road on a white horse and a borrowed saddle! And Dad did not dream that a man he had helped would help me, pray with me, offer me money, say kind things to me, encourage me. Dad did not dream all this would happen.

I got on Go West that morning and rode on toward the rising sun, rode on toward the east. And I said, "It does pay to be a Sunday school boy after all! It does pay to live for Christ. It sure does and I am going to live for God and I am going to be a preacher." What's more, I was confident that the dear Lord was going to take care of me in the days ahead just as He had taken care of me the night before.

The night I spent on that Texas ranch had a profound effect on me and in the days that have followed.

Good Neighbor, why don't you say, "Lord, I am going to serve you. I will follow you. I will be yours. I trust you to save me and forgive me of my sins and I am going to live for you. I am going to go where you want me to go and be what you want me to be."

Like the writer of Hebrews, we can say, *"...he that cometh to God must believe that he is, and that he is a rewarder of them that diligently seek him"* (Hebrews 11:6).

DANGER IS AN ANGRY BULL

THE BULL WAS BORN MAD AND BAD—AND DIED THE SAME WAY! MY ONLY COMPLAINT WAS—HE WANTED TO TAKE ME WITH HIM! WITH HIS HEAD DOWN AND HIS TAIL STRAIGHT OUT BEHIND—THE BIG BLACK BULL CHARGED!

Two years ago we were in desperate need of money and decided to sell our little herd of cattle. When we rounded them up we found there were six that would probably bring so little it would hardly pay us to send them to Nashville. These were three old white-faced cows and their small calves. Then there was one large half-Brahma cow with her black calf that got away and ran up on one of the mountains in the Big Pasture.

That big black cow was as wild as a deer and her bull calf was even wilder. He had been sired by a big Santa Gertrudis bull that we had slaughtered because he showed a tendency to fight.

So the bull calf certainly had plenty of fighting blood in his veins.

Cutting Him Out

For the next two years the black bull ran wild on the mountains and in the valleys of the Ranch while he was growing up. Then last spring we began buying a few cattle to start another herd. I asked Owen Layne, one of the best neighbors any man ever had, to buy some "bumping" heifers for me and he found me fifteen or sixteen.

(A "bumping" heifer is a young cow about to have her first calf. These sell cheaper than older cows because the first calf will not be as large as the succeeding one will be.)

I sure didn't want that black bull, with his hot fighting blood, to stay with these heifers and told the men we had better cut him out of the herd and put him in the East Pasture.

But this was easier said than done. I went back with a couple of the men one day and we located him easily. And we easily cut him out from the rest of the cattle and started him up toward the East Pasture. But we never did get him there.

At first he would try to run back to get with the other cattle and when we would head him off, he would simply stop and refuse to go any place. When we rode toward him, yelling and waving a rope, he would wait until we were almost on top of him before he would turn, run a few feet and then wheel to face us again.

Then he began running into the brush, using the same tactics. And it was harder to get to him when he was in the brush and sometimes he would high-tail it back for the Tee Pee Town clearing where the other cattle were. He soon found that he could not outrun the horses. When he got into the clearing we could always head him off. And then the whole thing would begin all over again.

Finally we got him about a quarter of a mile from the other cattle when he seemed determined not to move another inch. I pulled gun and fired it into the ground at his feet and, to my surprise, he didn't blink an eye!

He held his ground, pawing and tossing his head, until I holstered the gun and rode up to crack him across the nose with the end of my lariat.

He reluctantly turned and trotted a few feet and then whirled around to face me again.

Every time he found a thick place in the brush he would simply stop and sulk until one of us could get a horse in with him and make him move.

This began to get ridiculous—three cowboys who couldn't drive just one black bull!

But it was getting late and I called it off until the morning. I knew, anyway, we were going to have to change our tactics if we got the job done. Of course I could have roped him easily enough. But if I had roped him it would have meant a fight all the way to the East Pasture. And I do mean "fight" because that's exactly what he would have done. I didn't want Kamar to get cut up or bruised and, besides, it is no picnic dragging a bull three-quarters of a mile.

So I called it off until the next morning.

Drive 'Em All

The next morning I made two changes. First, I loaded my six-gun with tiny shot that ranchers often use to shoot mice with around the barn. These cartridges are not powerful enough to blow a hole in the wall. In fact, I doubt if you could even kill a mouse with them more than twelve or fifteen feet away.

The other change was that we no longer tried to drive the black bull by himself. We simply drove all of the little herd up to the ranch barns together.

As I had supposed, this was a great deal easier. Now, when we made him move, he moved into the small herd and kept going the same direction as they did.

And now when he went into the brush and stopped I would ride in behind him and sting him with the mouse-shot! Of course, with his thick skin, (remember, that's where your thick shoe soles come from!) I would have to be fairly close before he could even feel the shot.

We finally drove the cattle into the penning pasture and then into the field of one of the stallions.

As soon as we got all of them into this field we promptly drove all of them back out again—except for the black bull. Since the fence is prepared for the stallion, it is six and seven feet high and strong.

We drove the cattle back across the camp ground and then down the Old Pioneer Road into the Big Pasture.

I told the men to see that the bull got plenty of feed and water. I would decide later what to do with him.

"Later" Came Sooner Than I Had Expected!

It must have been about eight o'clock the next morning when one of the men rang the ranch phone on my desk. The black bull had torn a hole in the stallion's fence, he told me.

I picked up my six-gun and hurried out to the white Scout and drove up to the penning pasture.

Sure enough, there the bull was. He had left a gaping hole in the stallion's face where he had gone through like gravy through a paper napkin!

I got out of the Scout and walked over to the men. "Let's see if we can get him in the old corral," I said. "You men stay here and I will see if I can encourage him to come back down this way."

There was no time to saddle a horse. Any bull that could go through that stallion's fence would certainly have no trouble with the old fence around the penning pasture. And he plainly intended to leave then and there. As the bull walked steadily toward the old fence in the corner that he had been driven through the day before, I ran after him to see if I could head him off or, at least, attract his attention.

Well, I didn't head him off but I dead-sure did attract his attention!

When he saw me following, he really came alive. He whirled to face me, lowered his head, and began to paw the ground. I stopped and waited to see what he was going to do. Unlike some people I know, it didn't take him long to make up his mind!

With his head lowered he began moving, almost in a crouch, toward me. Then he began to pick up speed. With his head moving in a straight line toward me he began sidling—moving his hind end from one side to the other—in the way peculiar to many bulls when they are getting ready to charge.

There was no doubt in the world about it—this big fellow planned to clean my plow and polish it to the point!

I quickly looked around and my heart jumped right up into my throat. This bull really had me where the hair was short. I couldn't have been more nearly in the center of the penning pasture. It would be impossible for me to get to any fence before the black fellow caught me—and he knew it!

With his head down and his tail sticking straight out behind—the black bull charged!

Scared as I was, I had more sense than to run. I had my six-gun, loaded with mouse shot in my hand and I raised it and fired. Probably the tiny pellets did not even reach the bull at his point. But I thought the loud **bang** of the gun might discourage him.

But if this fellow was discouraged he had a real poker face and didn't show it.

On he came at full speed.

I fired again and this time felt sure some of the little pellets stung his face. But again, there was no reaction. If anything, he came faster.

For the third time I pulled the trigger and with exactly the same results. I was in a tight spot and I knew it. I had only three cartridges left of the tiny shot and the best I could hope to do with them was to bluff him.

Now he was almost upon me! I braced myself, decided to fire point blank in his face and them jump to the right side.

He was just a few feet away when I pulled the trigger the fourth time. The little shot hit him full in the face and the bull flinched his head slightly to one side and he flashed by me on the left!

I whirled but he did not stop or turn. Instead, I'll declare if he didn't run straight for the old corral and go in.

The excitement was over.

The End of the Black Bull

The men closed the gate of the corral while I stepped into the Scout and drove down to my house to pick up a Winchester rifle. I drove back to the old corral, got out of the Scout and joined the men by the fence.

The bull was on the far side of the corral, facing us, pawing the ground and daring us to fight!

I reached the Winchester to my shoulder and took aim. I had no choice. Where there are so many young people at the ranch every summer I simply cannot keep any dangerous animal around.

I pulled the trigger and the black bull dropped dead in his tracks.

A few minutes later I was again sitting at my desk in my office. From the time the men had first called to say the bull was out until now had only been about fifteen minutes. There had been some excitement but everything had turned out all right. (For me, I mean, not for the bull!)

But I realized that I had certainly been mighty close to serious injury or even death. Things could certainly have turned out much differently.

When the bull charged me I decided to fire in his face and then jump to my right. It happened that the bull flinched and swerved the other way.

But what would have happened if I, in the split second of decision, had jumped the other way! Or what if the bull had swerved the other way.

Instead of sitting at my desk I would probably be on the way to the hospital or even the morgue.

And I would not be the first man to meet serious injury or even death on the horns of a bull as hundreds of Texas graves could silently testify.

Make no mistake about it—danger is an angry black bull!

That Thin Invisible Line

There is often just a thin invisible line that separates well being from misfortune, triumph from tragedy, health from sickness and life from death.

Probably everyone of us have come close to death scores of times when we didn't even know it!

In December I spent a week preaching at the Sword Conference in the Highland Park Baptist Church of Chattanooga. One Thursday afternoon the Princess and I left Chattanooga for home. We had just left the city limits and were driving down the slopes of famous Lookout Mountain when highway patrolmen waved us to the side of the road. Just a head there had been a serious head-on collision between two automobiles and a man and woman had been killed and another man thought to be dying. We waited while ambulances loaded up the crash victims and sped away with them.

Both Cathy and I realized that, had we come along one minute earlier, it might well have been in front of us that the driver had carelessly directed his car. It could just as easily been us who were killed.

...I remember a midnight when I was driving down a Georgia highway. Ahead of me there was an underpass and on the other side a car was rapidly approaching. The other driver suddenly swerved far out on his right shoulder and struck the wall of the underpass. His car glanced off, spun around, hit the underpass on the other side and then came again all the way across the highway to crash into the right wall!

I jammed on my brakes and stopped perhaps one hundred feet before reaching the underpass. Of course I jumped out of my car and ran to the other driver.

His car, a white Cadillac convertible, had not turned over. But all four wheels had been knocked off and the body was dented and smashed all the way around.

The driver, without a single scratch on him, was still sitting behind the wheel, clumsily trying to start the car. He was so drunk it took him several minutes to realize what had happened.

As I stood with a flashlight that night, stopping cars on either side of the underpass while waiting for a wrecker, I sure did some serious thinking. What if we had met in that underpass? If I had been going just ten seconds faster or he ten seconds slower I would have been in there with him while he was bouncing from side to side!

I could fill up the pages of this entire book with stories such as these. I was driving in Tennessee on Labor Day when an oncoming driver evidently went insane and deliberately decided to kill someone. He crossed a four-lane highway to crash head long into a car ahead of me. He was killed and so were a doctor and two nurses in the car he crashed into.

But it could just as easily have been my car that he selected.

Now, in none of these instances was I saved because of any skill whatsoever on my part. Humbly speaking it "just happened" that my life was spared.

But, Good Neighbor, it is not any "happen so" that you are alive this very minute. You and I are both alive because of the goodness of God. In Psalm 103 David said, ***"Bless the LORD, O my soul, and forget not all his benefits...Who redeemeth thy life from destruction..."*** (Psalm 103:2 and 4a).

If you are well and strong and healthy, you certainly ought to thank God. Many others, exposed to the same disease germs that you were exposed to, died as a result! Many others may have been killed while walking down the same street, fishing in the same river or riding on the same bus system as you!

Do It Today

It seems to me that one of the most important questions of our lives should be, "What are we doing with the days God has given us?"

Moses had the right answer when he prayed, *"So teach us to number our days, that we may apply our hearts unto wisdom."* (Psalm 90:12)

We often think that wise people are the ones that have the best education, have the best jobs, have the most money, have the most political pull or something of the kind. But Daniel had a far better description of the truly wise person. He said,

"And they that be wise shall shine as the brightness of the firmament; and they that turn many to righteousness as the stars for ever and ever." (Daniel 12:3)

Good Neighbor, all of us are going to live somewhere forever and ever. Some, as Daniel said, *"to everlasting life, and some to shame and everlasting contempt."* This is of more concern to the Lord than anything else in all the world. It is a matter of such great concern that,

"...God so loved the world, that he gave his only begotten Son, that whosoever believeth in him should not perish, but have everlasting life." (John 3:16)

If you and I, then, would please God—we must be interested in winning others for Him. God has spared our lives and has given each of us some ability to help in the winning of the lost.

Do It Now

Do not salve your conscience with the thought that "sometime" you are going to help others for Christ. Right now is the time to begin doing what God wants you to do. After all, you do not know how much longer you will have to serve Him.

You and your black bull could swerve the same direction within the next sixty seconds!